To Stephen, with love

Heather
Esmé
Rnona

ANTARCTICA
The Last Horizon

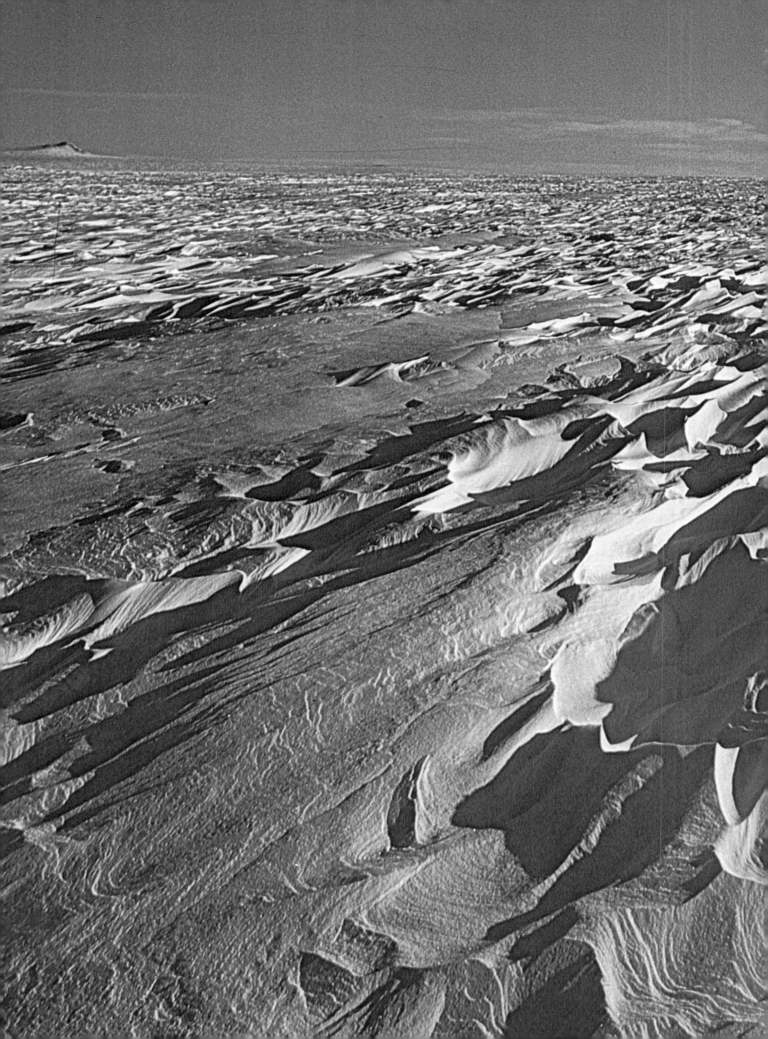

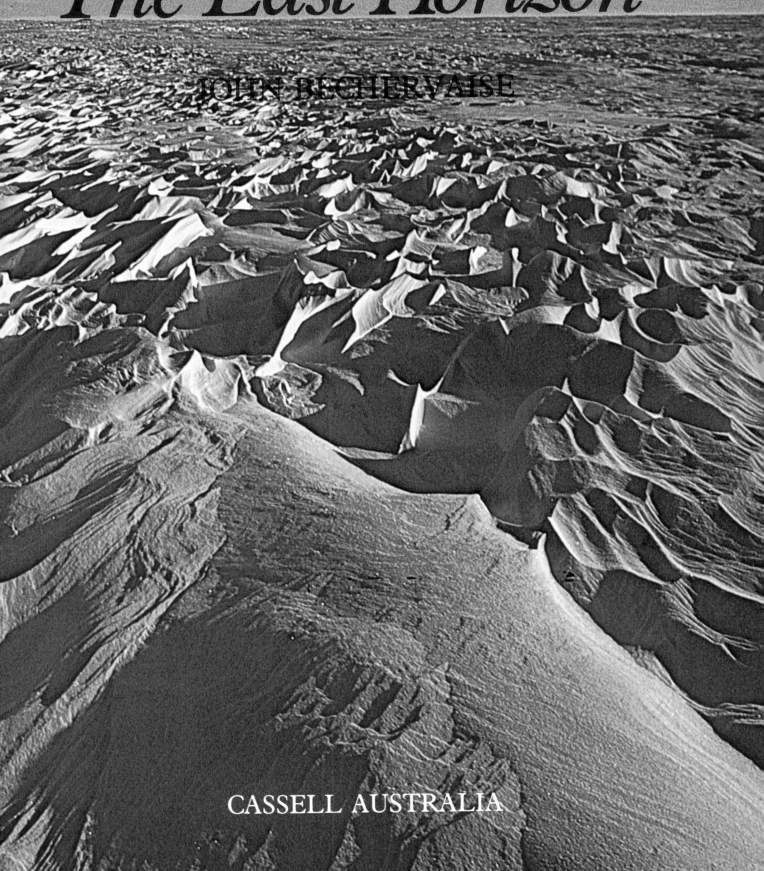

ANTARCTICA
The Last Horizon

JOHN BÉCHERVAISE

CASSELL AUSTRALIA

With gratitude, to P.G.L.
for opportunities made and given,
and to L.F.B.
for her encouragement

Conceived and produced by
Ian Green Books Pty Ltd for
Cassell Australia Limited
31 Bridge Road, Stanmore, New South Wales
30 Curzon Street, North Melbourne, Victoria
in association with Cassell Limited, Auckland

Copyright © John Mayston Béchervaise 1979
All rights reserved. No part of this publication
may be reproduced or transmitted in any form or by
any means, electronic or mechanical, including
photocopying, recording or by any information storage
and retrieval system, without permission in writing
from the publishers.

First published as *The Far South*, 1961
This completely revised and expanded edition
published by Cassell Australia Limited, 1979
Designed by Ian Green and Vicki Hamilton
Set in 10/12 point Plantin by
Monotrade Pty Ltd, Melbourne
Printed and bound by
Shanghai Printing Press Ltd, Hong Kong
F.979

National Library of Australia
Cataloguing in Publication Data
Béchervaise, John Mayston.
    Antarctica, the last horizon.

    Index.
    First published as The far south, Sydney: Angus
& Robertson, 1961.
    Bibliography.
    ISBN 0 7269 0474 0

    1. Antarctic regions. I. Title.

919.89

Acknowledgments

My sincere thanks are due to the men with whom I have shared all seasons of four years spent in the far south, principally at the Australian bases of Heard Island, Macquarie Island, Mawson and Davis; but also, at Mirni (USSR); McMurdo Sound, Byrd and Amundsen-Scott, at the South Pole (USA); and at Scott Base (NZ).

To my friends and colleagues of the Antarctic Division of the Australian Commonwealth Department of Science, I would like also to express thanks for valuable suggestions and expert advice over a quarter of a century.

Photographic acknowledgments

The majority of photographs, both in black and white and colour, were taken by the author over a period of twenty-five years (1953-77), during which he led three Australian National Antarctic Research Expeditions wintering in Antarctica, made numerous flights and cruises in the Antarctic and sub-Antarctic, observing the activities of several nations, and was Australian representative with the US Operation *Deep Freeze*, 1965-66, at McMurdo Sound, Byrd and South Pole.

Because Antarctica is a circum-polar continent, specific photographs are often typical of their latitude, and could represent scenes anywhere on their particular parallels. Pack ice, icebergs and shelf-ice, for instance, are similar in all sectors; the antarctic plateau is sastrugi-surfaced over millions of square kilometres; a glacier on Heard Island may be indistinguishable from one photographed, say, on South Georgia, while Macquarie Island or Kerguelen may be taken as typical of the sub-Antarctic islands outside the Antarctic Convergence. Photographs taken during expeditions from Mawson, MacRobertson Land, are not untypical of most of eastern Antarctica.

The author is indebted to the Antarctic Division of the Department of Science and the Environment (particularly for allowing the use of their ANARE photographs), to the RAAF, to the US Navy, and to many expedition men of the Antarctic Division, Melbourne whose names follow, and whose initials appear under the photographs they have contributed, all of which are gratefully acknowledged. I. Allison; G. Bradley; A. Brown; A. Campbell-Drury; M. Cutcliffe; W. J. R. Dingle; E. H. M. Ealey; F. W. Elliott; H. J. Evans; M. Fisher; G. Foote; H. Gehrke; K. Gooley; G. Hulme; P. G. Law; L. Le Guay; D. Linders; G. Newton; R. O'Leary; D. Parer; M. Prise; R. Reeves; R. Ruker; P. Shaw; I. Thomas; R. Thompson; J. Watts; G. Wheeler.

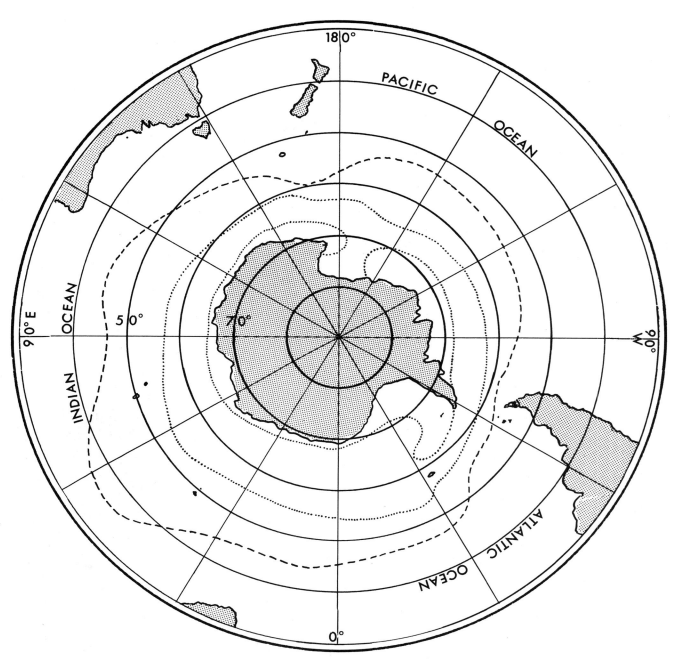

South latitudes: In this map the southern extensions of the Pacific, the Atlantic, and the Indian Oceans are seen to merge and form the frigid circumpolar Southern Ocean. New Zealand, and the southern coasts of Africa, Australia, and South America lie within the 30th parallel of south latitude, which forms the circumference of the map. Many scientists consider that the south coast of Aus- *tralia and that part of Antarctica directly facing it were once contiguous–part of the ancient hypothetical land-mass of Gondwanaland. The hatched line represents the approximate mean course of the West Wind Drift, virtually coinciding with the Antarctic Convergence. The two inner dotted lines mark the limits of pack ice, respectively in September and in March.*

Introduction

Antarctica is the highest, coldest, stormiest and driest continent on earth. It is an immense ice dome of more than 13 000 000 square kilometres overlying a rock mass much of which is depressed below sea-level by the sheer weight of ice. Just to compare it in size with other great continents—Europe (including the USSR as far east as the Ural Mountains), approximately 10 000 000 square kilometres; the United States of America, about 9 500 000 square kilometres; or with Australia, less than 8 000 000 square kilometres—is to understand why all nations, wealthy or undeveloped, are interested and concerned in its potential exploitation. To these generalities I add one most significant: from a satellite it is possible to see half the world, a hemisphere containing a total human population less than a quarter that of Europe. The view is dominated by Antarctica, and Australia.

For centuries it was curiosity, as much as zest for adventure and trade, that urged men to explore the far south. Today, though scientific curiosity concerning the polar regions has paid inestimable dividends, the Antarctic Continent and its surrounding oceans are known to hold resources of food and energy in quantities sufficient to stimulate universal activity and interest. Successful exploitation, however, will be fraught with immense problems if the vital conservation of the interdependent members of a highly specialized cycle of life, the antarctic marine ecosystem,[1] is to be restored and maintained.

More than two centuries have passed since Antarctica was isolated as a vast, frozen continent. For a century and a quarter after the continent's icy ramparts of berg and barrier had been circumnavigated, no one set foot on the place, all interest being reserved for coastal exploration and the wealth of the antarctic seas.

Then, with the close of the nineteenth century, there began the 'heroic age' of sledging over the most inhospitable tracts of the planet's surface. These probes, with

Chaos in the ice, caused by a fall from the coastal ice-cliffs.

3

dogs or ponies, or men alone in harness, reached the ashen heart of Antarctica and, not without tragedy, took a cross-section of its nature and hazards.

The second quarter of the twentieth century witnessed the beginning of a truly scientific approach with new logistics, the mechanization of equipment and transport, the setting up of instruments to calibrate the continent, to dispel the myths and to measure its effect, especially meteorologically, on the world at large. No longer did mapping depend on traversing the surface. Aircraft plotted the icy tracts and projecting mountains between broad, ever-expanding horizons.

In 1957–58, during the first decade of the century's third quarter, there occurred a world-wide scientific symposium with the object of investigating our planet and its spatial environment by studies nowhere more significant than in the Antarctic. Supported by the governments of the principal nations, the world-wide projects of this 'International Geophysical Year' (IGY) included the establishment of observatories, laboratories and living quarters, with necessary provisioning, radio facilities, power units and maintenance, at intervals round the entire coast of Antarctica and at selected inland sites including that of the South Pole. On the surface the Pole area, incidentally, had last been reached by Captain Scott who, with his companions, died on the homeward journey.

When we proceed through the decades leading towards the year 2000, as a direct result of the interest engendered by the research programmes of the IGY,

Gilded by the low sun a Weddell seal prepares to suckle her young.

Into the sunset. Dog team on sea-ice. [D.P.]

a new phase is apparent. Quite evidently the joint scientific research of the international stations had to be maintained, for its pursuit had revealed ever-expanding horizons as challenging as those beckoning to the physical explorers of the beginning of the century. So antarctic projects continue to receive the support and active encouragement of all civilized nations. Inevitably, subscribing governments, aware of the possible potential of Antarctica, in sources of energy, in minerals and, particularly, in food from the sea, are anxious to exploit these if and where practicable. The immediate future will certainly see such investigation intensified, we can only hope with the same sense of co-operation and courtesy as has been apparent in the research of nations participating in the IGY and signatory to the subsequent Antarctic Treaty.[2] This treaty guaranteed, for a period of at least thirty years, the use of Antarctica for peaceful purposes only, with freedom of access for scientific research, general exploration and for the study of antarctic fauna and flora; other provisions concerned conservation, the prohibition of nuclear explosions and the holding in abeyance of existing territorial claims. However, while scientific knowledge is intrinsically indivisible and, like solar energy, is ultimately available to all, the harvesting and mining of the earth has traditionally been national, exclusive and divisive.

In recent years there has been a development of antarctic tourism, in a popular way, especially for passengers on non-stop return flights from Australia and

Statuesque group of emperor penguins at Cape Crozier, Ross Island.

The tranquil pack. An iceberg, calved from the continent, amidst typical pack ice.

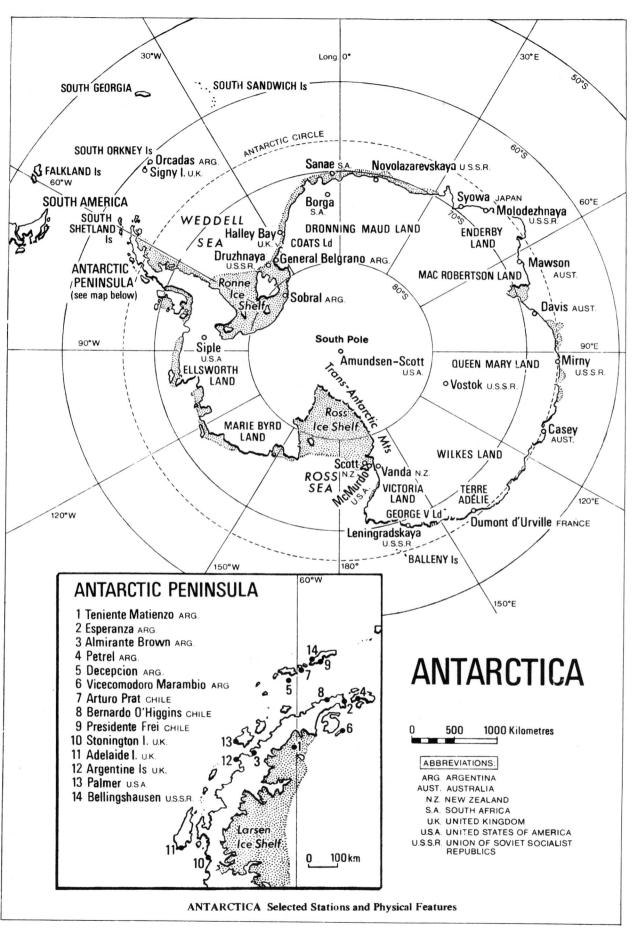

ANTARCTICA

ANTARCTIC PENINSULA

1 Teniente Matienzo ARG.
2 Esperanza ARG.
3 Almirante Brown ARG.
4 Petrel ARG.
5 Decepcion ARG.
6 Vicecomodoro Marambio ARG
7 Arturo Prat CHILE
8 Bernardo O'Higgins CHILE
9 Presidente Frei CHILE
10 Stonington I. U.K.
11 Adelaide I. U.K.
12 Argentine Is U.K
13 Palmer U.S.A.
14 Bellingshausen U.S.S.R.

0   500   1000 Kilometres

0   100km

ABBREVIATIONS:
ARG. ARGENTINA
AUST. AUSTRALIA
N.Z. NEW ZEALAND
S.A. SOUTH AFRICA
U.K. UNITED KINGDOM
U.S.A. UNITED STATES OF AMERICA
U.S.S.R. UNION OF SOVIET SOCIALIST
REPUBLICS

ANTARCTICA Selected Stations and Physical Features

Used with permission of New Zealand Antarctic Society

New Zealand. Successful cruises have also been demonstrated. With so many projections on our cinema and television screens of the astonishing beauty of Antarctica and of its unique wildlife, and by the increased interest in the literature of the far south, further popular demand is inevitable. Tourism will continue and, provided the necessary ecological safeguards are observed, it will provide enrichment to the lives of many fortunate voyagers. Tourist accommodation could be provided if such a development were economically viable.[3] Douglas Mawson certainly envisaged this more than fifty years ago. All-weather flight facilities are practicable in several localities, with ferrying flights to selected tourist destinations, probably by movable-winged aircraft.

Amongst the most rewarding experiences of a life largely given to exploration, not always in a physical and geographical sense, are those summers and winters I have spent in various parts of Antarctica. To witness the marvellous cycle of seasonal changes between the periods of the midnight sun and of the noon darkness is to be uniquely conscious of the movements of the earth, in its orbit and upon its axis, and at times to reach out into space, to brilliant stars beyond the pale draperies of the aurora. Antarctica provides ideal conditions for the investigation of geomagnetism, cosmic radiation, the ionosphere and of other events outside the range of our direct perception. The instruments which serve as intermediaries between these events and our assessment of them, in the polar solitudes may seem an extension of our minds. They count impulses and trace graphs, they describe inevitable curves, and they reveal evidence of storms and calms otherwise beyond our apprehension. There are times during daylong dawns and sunsets or nightlong displays of the aurora, racing and waving across the stars, when one might indeed fancy he heard Plato's inaudible music of the spheres.

There have been times when the sight and sound of birds have alone seemed worth the expenditure of an entire year in the remotest, coldest places on earth. Albatrosses tending their young in ancestral nests between the hanging glaciers of Heard Island; minute storm petrels adrift in an infinity of blizzard snow; stately emperor penguins trumpeting over the polished

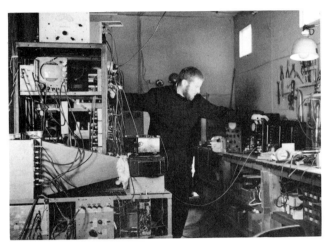

Radar equipment for upper atmosphere physics. [G.N.]

A good team. The teamster is an Australian, E. L. Macklin.

sea-ice black against the light of the unrising sun; any of these may fill a memory as long as life. To stand on the frozen ocean in the apricot light of the midnight sun, watching a Weddell seal suckle her young at the foot of ice-cliffs as high as steeples or, in winter, to watch her surfacing at a pool kept open by her gnawing through the two metres of ice everywhere else plating the sea; these hapenings, too, are still amongst the wonders of the world. Even when all visible and audible life seems mythical, there may be the unbelievable sight of icebergs converted to gigantic opals, or of a sea of sastrugi[4] waves—the wind chiselled surface of inland areas larger than France—each tipped with gold and turquoise shaded, or streaming with drift snow like blown silver hair.

Even when the air is dark with blizzard, and one flounders along a rope guideline from hut to hut, or lies in a down cocoon preserving the warmth that is life, there are new dimensions of time, and new boundaries to one's sensory perceptions.

Light blizzard drift, Antarctic mainland. Such rocky areas as this, near Mawson, are unusual.

Penguins at Cape Crozier, destination of the historic winter journey by Wilson, Bowers and Cherry-Garrard in 1911.

Harbour and plateau: Mawson station stands on a rocky area between the rising ice of the plateau and the frozen harbour.

For a million years—the period, probably, of the present glaciation—almost the whole surface of that land has lain beneath an overburden of ice thousands of metres thick. It revolves round the South Pole like a hub-cap of our planet, separated from the inhabited lands by the world's loneliest oceans. Its discovery and exploration were difficult, often dangerous, and generally uncomfortable. It is a fascinating story for the beginnings

Mountains of Victoria Land are visible 100 kilometres away across the Ross Ice Shelf in this picture taken from near Cape Crozier.

A large Adélie penguin rookery at Cape Adare, Ross Sea (170°E.).

of which we much retrace time and dream, with the old philosophers and geographers, of a fabled *Terra Australis* or Great South Land. We shall follow the journeys of men who conquered their fear of endless empty oceans and utter loneliness and, to replace fancy and fiction, charted the limits of two unknown continents.

The antarctic plateau that rises abruptly from the sea is twice the average height of mountainous Asia. It is, for the most part, a lifeless desert of ice and snow where the temperatures remain perpetually below freezing point. Not even the lichens (belonging to primitive orders of flowerless plants), that in summer brighten the coastal rocks, can survive, except in the most sheltered crevices, more than a few kilometres inland. Antarctica's story would be incomplete without discussion of nature's prolonged and constant efforts to maintain life in its surrounding seas. The most familiar symbol of Antarctica is a penguin, the creature which, in order to sustain life through millions of years of slow climatic change, evolved wings for flight under water, and blubber to insulate it from temperatures too low for any other bird on earth. How does the northern Arctic differ from these southern polar regions, apart from being the only natural haunt of the white polar bear? Why are there neither Eskimos nor bears in the Antarctic, nor any parallel forms of life?

In the Antarctic there are grey weeks of morose howling blizzard when the air is opaque with minute streaming particles of snow—when literally one may lean on the wind—and there are days of extraordinary silence,

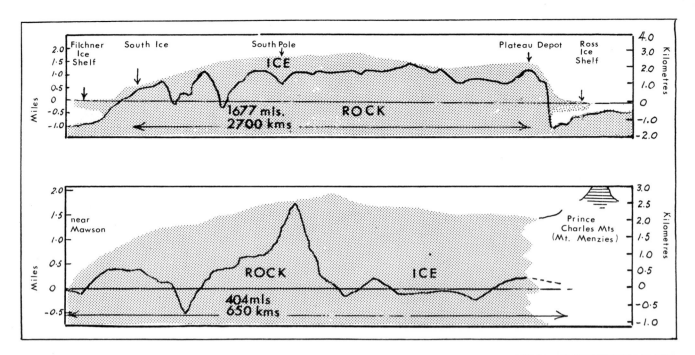

Rock beneath the ice. Two typical rock profiles, obtained by seismic sounding. The upper figure sketches a trans-antarctic profile, obtained by the Commonwealth Trans-Antarctic Expedition 1957–58. Simultaneous gravity measurements showed anomalies. The lower figure, on a much larger scale, shows the result of an Australian traverse south of Mawson, also made during the International Geophysical Year. It will be seen from both profiles that the ice along the line of these traverses rises almost three kilometres above sea-level; also that, in places, it rests on rock below sea-level.

IGY co-operation: a Russian visit to Mawson, the senior Australian base: Left to right: K. Peake-Jones; the author, then leader of the ANARE at Mawson; Captain Alexander Dubinin, master of the Ob, and Professor Maximov.

of brilliant light and of air so clear that nothing is hidden except by crests of ice or the curvature of the earth. Abrupt mountain ranges, bleak and bare beyond description, thrust through kilometres of ice. Wind-blown snow streaming past their summits in immeasurable quantities is always too cold and dry to adhere to their rock. Why is the weather so different from that of the inhabited continents? Why is there continuous daylight in summer for months on end, with corresponding periods of winter gloom? Of what rocks are the harsh mountains formed? What is the cause of the deep dark cracks in the ice which we call crevasses? And how on earth did such an enormous mantle of ice ever get there in the first place? We must answer many questions of this kind.

It does seem odd, on the face of it, that, in spite of all the accounts of discomforts and dangers, there has never been a time when more men have ventured, through stormy seas and drifting bergs and pack ice, to Antarctica. The station at the South Pole itself has been functioning continuously since its components were air-dropped, and it was set up for observations during the IGY; an Australian base at Mawson has maintained regular observations night and day since 1954; there was UK activity on the Antarctic Peninsula before that. Still British, Argentine, Chilean, French, Japanese, New Zealand, South African bases, and those of the USA and the USSR, number at least thirty, all

maintaining continuing research into the nature of the earth and its atmosphere; of the energies that govern our existence, including those emanating from within and without the bounds of our solar system. A modern account of the 'great white south' must speak of aspects of science unknown, no less than of territories unexplored, at the beginning of the twentieth century, and use many terms then uncoined.

In this volume I shall hope to share an essential journey. First we may experience something of the nature of the quest through the accounts of the earliest mariners who proved Antarctica's existence; then, through successive phases of our twentieth century exploration—heroic, logistic, scientific and economic—into the probable future of the last continent. Particularly we must consider the balance of the antarctic ecosystem,[5] already so disturbed by the mass killing of whales and, currently, by the trawling of krill[6] and scalefish. Man, of course, by his being the most successful animal, will continually modify earlier states of ecological balance; yet, beyond certain limits, he does so at his peril, endangering the existence of species and even his own place in nature.

Throughout our long journey there must be pauses, times when we halt to perceive strange, beautiful and even terrible phenomena on the margins of human experience. What is there in Antarctica beyond the calls of pure science and adventure which, one trusts, will always be answered wherever they are to be heard? What else may eventually make the least hospitable region on earth of importance to mankind? Must men and women experience and combat odds, in the final analysis, as a human gesture?

The wandering albatross nests solitarily, although nests may be visible from each other. The solitary chick requires a year's nourishment before flying from its birthplace.

Adélie penguins on eggs, Cape Hallett, Ross Sea. Note the 'nests' of piled stones. [US NAVY]

The massive dome of Heard Island.

The Search for Antarctica

It is always pleasing to our sense of order when we have clear beginnings and endings in history; they make it so much easier to fill in the gaps and trace developments in a proper time scale. The need for order is probably the real reason why, in accounts of exploration in the southern hemisphere, old Greek fancies and early mediaeval superstitions supporting the presence of a great continent to balance the landmasses of Europe and Asia are so often mentioned. After all, once the idea of a spherical earth had occurred to men about two and a half thousand years ago, the filling in of blank spaces was bound to occur. To the Greeks empty wastes of sea would seem illogical. Even in fairly modern times it was fashionable to cover unexplored areas on the maps of 'dark' continents like Africa and Australia with pictures of birds and beasts and natives in strange guises. The famous map showing the voyage of van Neck to the East Indies as late as 1600 depicts a great sagacious elephant bestriding *Terra Australis Incognita* just where our modern Cape York is clearly visible and recognizable.

Aristotle (384–322 B.C.) considered the world a globe and Eratosthenes of Cyrene, a hundred years later, is credited with the invention of a system of latitude and longitude for his maps. He also held the earth to be spherical, and this hypothesis, doubtless based on the circular shadow of the earth at the moon's eclipse, remained amongst the wise at least until the time of the great geographer Ptolemy, who lived in Alexandria about the year A.D. 150. By then Europe, the Mediterranean and Africa were all known more or less clearly (it is fairly certain that Africa had been rounded by the Phoenecians, although Ptolemy doesn't show this). It was natural that on representations of the globe the landmasses of the old world should be 'balanced' by hypothetical lands beyond the Pillars of Hercules in the west, and in the far south.

All these rich theories and speculations slept nearly a thousand years through the dark ages following the decline of Rome and her great empire. They were awakened during the early Renaissance by tales of the remarkable journeys of the Polos—Marco, his father Nicolo, and his uncle Maffeo—all of whom returned to their native Venice towards the end of the year 1295 after an absence of twenty-five years spent in China and in journeying to and from the court of Kublai Khan. They had visited Tibet, India, Burma, Malaya, Persia and even the coasts of Sumatra. Polo's tales were exaggerated and misunderstood; they were used freely to support men's fondest hopes. Eventually, of course, many of the old theories and accounts of the ancient world also came to light to buttress the prevailing spirit of inquiry.

It is likely that in the meantime Norse longboats had reached America and there had been wide voyaging by Polynesians in the Pacific. These were entirely outside our cultural stream and have only been appreciated in modern times. Still, it is just possible that rumours of such exploits, hopelessly distorted, travelled across Asia and down through Europe with the bearers of carved walrus tusks, or up from the East Indies with the Polos.

H.M.S. Challenger *amidst icebergs and floe-ice, February 1874.*

The centuries pass and Vasco da Gama and Magellan make for us a newer, more definite, starting point in modern geographical discovery. Africa was turned (1497) and the world was circumnavigated (1519–22). In recent years the outstanding voyages of the Portuguese have become more familiar as a result of research into old maps of astonishing provenance.[7] There is not doubt that the 'Dauphin' map, presented to the British Museum in 1790 by Sir Joseph Banks, represented in its own cartographical convention the eastern and southern coasts of Australia all the way from Cape York to Cape Otway. Dated about 1536 it precedes Cook's charts by well over 200 years. And there are other sixteenth century maps which were jealously guarded as 'classified' information but, fortunately, were sometimes illegally copied and preserved, notably in Dieppe, from such disruptions and calamities as the Spanish 'captivity' of Portugal (1580–1640) and the Lisbon earthquake and fire of 1755.

Always beyond the southern limits of the intrepid voyages charted by these mediaeval maps, there persisted in the minds of men a great unknown continent. It was generally assumed to be necessary by cartographers following the Ptolemaic philosophy and, not infrequently, its imaginary coast was vaguely delineated by them. Magellan's Tierra del Fuego, south of his stormy strait, was estimated by him to extend southward as the great continent but as such it lasted only fifty years, until Drake was driven far to the south in 1577 and sighted Cape Horn, where the Atlantic and Pacific oceans freely mingled, with nothing visible southward beyond.

In 1605 the mystical Fernandez de Quiros set sail with the blessing of Philip III of Spain to explore the coasts of *Terra Australis* (wherever they might be!). He reached the New Hebrides (later so-named by Cook), about which he made extravagant claims, stubbornly asserting that islands were continents, and took possession, on behalf of his king and his Church, of all

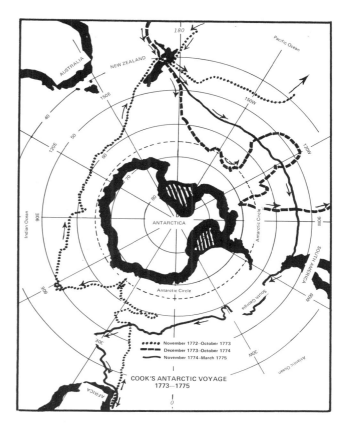

COOK'S ANTARCTIC VOYAGE
1773---1775

A disintegrating iceberg, afloat but held from drifting by heavy winter ice. This iceberg turned over and eventually was fragmented and carried away, returning to the ocean water which fell as snow thousands of years ago. [G.B.]

Captain James Cook. [courtesy The British Museum]

15

land southward in the world, naming it *Austrialia del Espiritu Santo*. Torres, who had been with de Quiros, sailed westward when his captain's vessel, perhaps suffering mutiny, returned to Peru. He passed between New Guinea and Australia and so further reduced the possible bounds of *Terra Australis*, although, in fact, his discoveries did not become known for many years.

Dutch navigators bound for the East Indies, and an occasional British freebooter—Dirck Hartog, Pelsaert, Nuyts, Tasman, Dampier are just a few voyagers who were also of particular significance to Australia—either on course or off, still further curtailed the boundaries, if not the hopes, of the desired continent. Tasman, by sailing south of New Holland (Australia) in 1642, thrust the possible northern limits of additional southern land thousands of kilometres beyond those imagined by de Quiros. However, having touched Tasmania, he discovered the western coasts of New Zealand and considered that they might be part of a continent stretching south and east. His second voyage, however, only confirmed the current Dutch opinions of New Holland—a bare, barbarous, unpleasant and unprofitable place. Nor was William Dampier impressed in 1688 and 1699.

His and the Dutch views remained current until Cook observed, with somewhat greater enthusiasm, the eastern coast of Australia between April and August in 1770, soon after he had disproved New Zealand's connection with any larger landmass. So extraordinarily successful was this voyage of Captain Cook that he was commissioned by the British Government to venture south again in order to settle, once and for all, whether any other continents existed in the Antipodes. A further

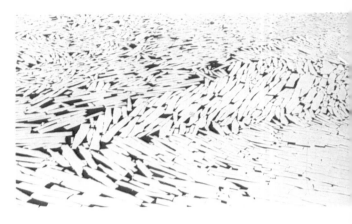

Young sea-ice, fractured by a storm, shows an unusual plank-like formation. An aerial view from about 750 metres.

The ice-foot. Adhering to the coast, and composed of frozen spray, drift and ice fragments, there is often a flat platform a little above highest tide, an area frequently useful for travelling, unloading stores, etc.

Coastal ice-cliffs. The greater part of the entire perimeter of Antarctica meets the sea in such cliffs as these.

task was to forestall the French who, at least since Bouvet's discoveries in 1738–39—when he saw seals and penguins, probably on the island (lat. 54°S., long. 5°W.) which now bears his name—had taken a great interest in the possibilities of an empire in the south. The gallant Bougainville was ahead of Cook; also poor Kerguelen, who, rather like de Quiros, thought his desolate islands in the sub-antarctic Indian Ocean were part of a new El Dorado; and there was Marion du

The forerunner. A solitary Adélie penguin, the first to arrive of many millions. Each year between October and March the Adélies return to the coastal islands of Antarctica for breeding.

Pressure cracks in sea-ice, forming radial patterns round coastal rocks.

Fresne also busy in the same sector of the cold south seas.

On his second voyage (1772–75) Cook circumnavigated the world in high southern latitudes. In a series of magnificent probes he established that no land could possibly exist to bridge the temperate and frigid zones of the hemisphere.

It would be difficult to imagine a task of such magnitude being done more thoroughly or more doggedly. Anyone who knows the pack ice and icebergs of the Antarctic must marvel at the tenacity of Cook. His *Resolution* (469 tonnes) and the even smaller *Adventure* (under Tobias Furneaux), with about two hundred men, not only crossed the Antarctic Circle (lat. 66° 32'S.) for the first time (17 January 1773) but, though constantly rebuffed by ice, headed southward beyond this latitude twice more during the next summer. I have voyaged through antarctic waters several times in what were thought small vessels, but the least of these, the Norwegian *Tottan*, was 550 tonnes, of steel, with powerful diesel engines, a radio voice to speak with the world and a radar eye to scan the dark or distant

Islands and icebergs near the Vestfold Hills: long. 78°E.

dangers of the sea. And, when we rolled through an arc of ninety degrees in storms and saw the merciless cliffs of great icebergs, I thought of Cook and others whose sole salvation lay in faith, courage and seamanship, whose sole power was from wind and current.

Cook's first meeting with the ice, after five stormy months in the Atlantic, was almost directly south of Africa. That year the pack ice must have extended unusually far to the north, and before Cook reached a latitude of 51°S. (the corresponding parallel in the northern hemisphere cuts through the south of England!) he was faced by ice-floes in every direction. He retired northwards, returned to the attack, and celebrated Christmas still making seaway amongst the icebergs. At his furthest south in this operation he was only a few hundred kilometres due west of where the Australian research station of Mawson was established a hundred and eighty-one years later. Had ice conditions forced Cook to make his probe only a little more to the west he might well have reached the antarctic continent, for he was already further south than the three hundred kilometre bulge of Enderby Land.

It must be remembered that Cook had no way of knowing whether the tremendous ice-fields heaving and scraping against his wooden hull were, somewhere in the misty distance, backed by land. His surmise was that land 'wholly covered' by ice that had been there 'from the earliest time' existed to his southward. And he was, as we now know, absolutely right. In most parts of Antarctica ice-cliffs, indistinguishable from the flat icebergs they spawn, are the only coastline. If Cook had sighted the long white line in the distance, either by direct vision through the incredibly clear atmosphere that is sometimes present, or by the fantastic optical illusions of the polar mirage, nothing could have afforded him any clue to its true identity. Even John Biscoe, the whaler, who, in 1831, discovered the land Cook so narrowly missed, and named it after his employers, the Enderbys, in fact approached the coast no more closely than forty or fifty kilometres; and was not certain, even then, whether his Enderby Land was part of the antarctic mainland.

After the exploration of antarctic ice in the African sector, Cook searched for Kerguelen's Land and the islands of Marion. He did not find them, which at least proved that Kerguelen's eager dreams of having discovered a vast domain for France would never materialize. Circumnavigation is, obviously, the only way of defining any land mass big or small. The Îles de Kerguelen seem vast when viewed from the sea, especially as their rugged coastline and high mountains emerge from the frequent mists. I have often looked through the eyes of Yves de Kerguelen-Trémarec at the lonely snow-covered peaks and required no great imagination to see them ranging away over a clouded continent. I often used to wonder just how close Cook sailed to the forlorn grey ice-cap of Heard Island, where I wintered and spent a year in charge of a sub-antarctic research station. That island had been discovered and forgotten a couple of times before Captain Heard

sighted it in 1853. The seas of the fifties of south latitude are the most tempestuous in the world, and the storm barrier there has been the first hazard of antarctic exploration in every period.

The great English navigator took his vessels south again to the sixtieth parallel and did not leave high latitudes until he turned their bows for New Zealand and the imaginary *Australia del Espiritu Santo* of de Quiros, which, naturally, he didn't find. The fixing of longitude in Cook's day, and for many subsequent decades, depended, of course, on the accuracy of a chronometer carried all the way from the vessel's home port. If its rate varied there was no means of correction, though it could, of course, be compared with another instrument. Latitude, however, depending on the sun's noon altitude—its daily maximum in a given place—is obtained by direct observations with a sextant, and presents no great difficulty.

After spending a southern winter in the Pacific, amongst the ever-fascinating south sea islands (which, eventually, on 14 February 1779, claimed his life), Cook made further polar journeys. First he crossed the Antarctic Circle again, in December 1773, having been in contact with ice, off and on, for about sixteen hundred kilometres of the voyage. He thrust on amidst the pack ice until it again seemed madness, but Cook left the grey icebergs only for a month, in order to make quite sure that there was no south Pacific continent between his present route and that of his 1769 voyage; then he returned south with magnificent resolution.

The second Pacific probe took him further south than ever before, to lat. 71° 10′S., in long. 106° 54′W. (about directly south of Easter Island, which he later visited), on 30 January 1774. The vessels then abutted massed floes ranging beyond the southern horizon. It was at this time that Cook wrote, most memorably:

I will not say it was impossible any where to get farther to the South; but the attempting of it would have been a dangerous and rash enterprise, and what, I believe, no man in my situation would have thought of. It was, indeed, *my* opinion, as well as the opinion of most on board, that this ice extended quite to the pole, or perhaps joined some land, to which it had been fixed from the earliest time. . . . And yet I think there must be some (land) to the South behind the ice; but if there is, it can afford no better retreat for birds, or any other animals, than the ice itself, with which it must be wholly covered. I, who had ambition not only to go farther than any one had been before, but as far as it was possible for man to go, was not sorry at meeting with this interruption, as it, in some measure, relieved us; at least, shortened the dangers and hardships inseparable from the navigation of the southern polar regions. Since therefore we could not proceed one inch farther to the South, no other reason need be assigned for my tacking and standing back to the North . . .[8]

Not for another fifty years was Cook's latitude surpassed, and then it was by another British navigator, James Weddell, who had been with the navy that Cook had served.

The third January of this magnificent voyage again saw Cook in the Antarctic after a second wintering in the Pacific (it was during this period that, as the New Hebrides, he renamed simply and suitably the grandiose *Austrialia* of de Quiros). This time he rounded Cape Horn from the west, annexed South Georgia and discovered the South Sandwich Islands in the Atlantic sector. There remained no part of the southern hemisphere that could possibly hold unknown continents. Cook has been hailed as the discoverer of Australia, which is, of course, an honour he would never have withheld from the Dutch and Portuguese (incidentally, it seems unlikely that he was familiar with the 'Dauphin' map); it is far odder, really, that he has not been given sufficient credit for discovering Antarctica. Two contestants for that honour whose names are often cited—Edward Bransfield and Nathaniel Palmer—never sailed anything like so far south as Cook, nor, any more than their successors for many years, did they set foot on the antarctic mainland. But, in following up Cook's reports of extensive seal colonies in antarctic islands, they did apparently both sight the tip of the Antarctic Peninsula, outside the Antarctic Circle. Until recently all surveys, aerial and surface, seemed to prove the peninsula part of the antarctic mainland, but ice-depthing soundings have now revealed that this section is separated from the main continental mass by ice extending well below sea-level. If for some the Antarctic Peninsula has lost status by being declared a large island of a group comprising much of the Pacific sector, the field is extended for those who would seek the first true landfall of the continental coast.

Cook wrote in another famous passage describing Antarctica:

Lands doomed by Nature to perpetual frigidness; never to feel the warmth of the sun's rays; whose horrible and savage aspect I have not words to describe. Such are the lands we have discovered; what then may we expect those to be, which lie still farther to the South? . . . If anyone should have resolution and perseverance to clear up this point by proceeding farther than I have done, I shall not envy him the honour of the discovery; but I will be bold to say, that the world will not be benefited by it.[9]

We must try to bridge the gap between Cook's time and our own, and discover just why men and women have turned their backs on safety and comfort and continued to dare storm and iceberg and sea-ice. Of more than a century I must write briefly for, although voyage after voyage was made in antarctic waters, each one served only to augment the discoveries of Cook, without modifying his basic theory of a great ice-sheathed continent, inaccessible and forbidding. Each journal retells much of Cook's original story; each chart delineates only a little that is new and certain. Slowly the continental ice-cliffs cease to recede as the vagaries of season permit men to sail further south here or there; never is there any assurance in 'the pack'. Always there is caprice, in season and in ice—for modern ice-breakers and steel ships strengthened to penetrate the floes, with their relatively vast power, as with the *Resolution* and the *Adventure*, stout sailing vessels of wood.

Before speeding forward through time to the Antarctica of the ageing twentieth century, let us consider some encounters which further defined the problems of the south. We may then be in a better position to realize that the powers of weather and ice, in spite of advances in technology, are still as capricious and capable of dealing disaster as in the days of Cook or Balleny, Scott or Mawson. In one sense all antarctic explorers are contemporary, for the continent they visit does not change in man's scale of time; and our modern mastery over space often seems merely to make more comprehensible the vastness and loneliness of the antarctic plateau and the polar seas.

Collision of the Erebus *and* Terror, *13 March, 1842 (from drawing by J. E. Davis).*

There are volatile aspects to all ways of life. In man's time ships, aircraft and surface vehicles change; the winds and the waves and the harsh crevassed surfaces of Antarctica do not. Man is better insulated because of improved clothing, vehicles and buildings, and these will continually be modified to his benefit, but explorers and scientists still may not trifle with the elements, nor cease from constant vigilance.

I do not want to trace in detail all the expeditions, great and small, or the odd ventures and voyages that, after James Cook, accomplished little or much, towards clarifying our knowledge of Antarctica. This has often been attempted and I shall list sufficient references at the end of this book for you to cover the ground more completely if you wish. In the literature there are numerous accounts of specific events which must be read unabridged if they are fully to be appreciated. I shall confine myself, in this section, to the broad canvas, dwelling briefly on the highlights, which reveal the pattern of antarctic discovery more clearly than a precise chronological account.

On 16 February 1875, exactly one hundred years after Cook steered north from the pack ice for the last time, the first steam-powered vessel to cross the Antarctic Circle,[10] HMS *Challenger*, still voyaged in mysterious waters. For one thing, observers on board could find no trace of the continent reported in 1840 in those parts by the explorer Charles Wilkes; yet from the sea-floor were dredged up rocks that proved beyond doubt that such a continent must exist beyond the horizon. The coastline in that area remained a phantom for many years after Wilkes's voyage. Though he must surely have been mistaken about the nature and position of his reported coasts, that he sighted land is certain, and his integrity is undoubted. There were certainly, in Wilkes's day, immense difficulties of travel in polar seas, quite apart from the hazards of ice and exposure. For mirages lifted white lands above the horizon, then as now (as I have myself seen many times when sledging on sea ice), and men could not believe their eyes; chronometers were subjected to low temperatures with unknown results; there were no radio time-signals to enable a navigator to be quite certain of his longitude.[11] Aeroplanes, to discover ways through the pack ice ahead of the ship and to examine and photograph the coast and establish its nature indisputably, from vertically above, were still far away—beyond the date of 16 November 1928 when Sir Hubert Wilkins made the first antarctic flight. Just imagine! Within a month he had flown poleward one thousand kilometres in a single day and seen much more of the Antarctic Peninsula than anyone in history.

The *Challenger*, in three and a half years cruising one hundred thousand kilometres, was undertaking a scientific investigation of the oceans of the world, foreshadowing the essential global approach of modern geophysics.

It was not science, however, that motivated antarctic exploration during most of the nineteenth century. Captain Cook had reported innumerable seals at South

The edge of the ice barrier. Although such ice fronts are afloat with between one-sixth and one-seventh only visible above the surface of the sea, they are often deeply undercut and extremely dangerous to approach.

Coastal rock. The haunt of the snow petrels.

Eroded iceberg. Over this grounded iceberg the furrows which once denoted coastal crevassing have been eroded to deep channels which, eventually, may become lines of fracture.

The upper layers in some icebergs, representing the deposits of several successive seasons, are here apparent. The lower layers are more compacted and may be scarcely visible where the névé has become solid ice.

The opalescent iceberg. There are frequently scenes of such tranquillity in the pack ice.

Georgia; the first indication that the antarctic oceans supported a rich fauna, and, within three or four years, British adventurers had begun to hunt them with great profit. The skins of fur seals were always in great demand in both Europe and Asia and for many years the exact sources of the most prolific supplies were jealously guarded secrets. As the seal population on Cook's South Georgia and the South Sandwich Islands fell, efforts were made to discover new rocky coasts that might buttress the lucrative trade. At the same time the value of the oil from other species, especially the ponderous elephant seal, became apparent.

In time with this British mercantile activity, but by no means in consort, moved that of the American sealers and whalers, including Edmund Fanning and Nathanial Palmer, both men of great intrepidity and enterprise. They were proud of the youthful independence of their country (1776), and the 'second' war of 1812–14 served to increase the spirit of rivalry between Britain and America which obscured and confused movements and discoveries in the early part of the century. While great cargoes of manageable sealskins for Canton remained the ambition of many, cumbersome whales and massive elephant seals were also hunted relentlessly. Early New England accounts record that the average yearly harpoonings of right whales over a long period exceeded ten thousand. In recent times there has been a running controversy, sometimes heated and acrimonious, about the priorities of discoveries in this era. At the time, however, many sightings of forlorn coasts under dangerous conditions of fog, swell and ice would not have been considered significant unless the areas were worth subsequent revisiting for the sake of their seal colonies, and hence the discoveries were kept secret. Logs were as sketchy and charts as fragmentary as safety allowed, but rumours and hopes were limited only by the love of adventure and the greatness of hearts. The idea of conserving the rich biomass, of 'farming' rather than 'mining' the wealth of the southern oceans in high latitudes in those days would have seemed as extravagant as unnecessary.

The South Shetland Islands, ice outliers of a suspected continent, had been discovered by an Englishman, William Smith, in February 1819. In the next year Edward Bransfield, RN, was despatched by naval authorities to determine whether the land seen was actually insular or continental. Smith was with him as pilot. The vessel, the brig *Williams* (used in both 1819 and 1820), charted the islands for two months, and there can be little doubt that what was eventually proved to be the main mass of Antarctica was sighted in lat. 64°S. (long. 60°W.) on 30 January 1820 and named Trinity Land. Bransfield explored with an outlook and in a manner wholly in the naval and scientific traditions of Cook, traditions which have never died and, on memorable occasions since, have inspired some of the finest expeditions.

Ten months after Bransfield's visit the American sealer Nathanial Palmer, in his tiny sloop *Hero* (44 tonnes), moving independently of Pendleton's sealing fleet anchored at Livingston Island, a hundred and sixty kilometres to the north, saw land in the same parts. An American account of all this, published in 1833, describes also the surprise meeting between Captain Palmer and the Russian explorer Captain Fabian von Bellingshausen in the South Shetlands. Not unnaturally, Bransfield is not mentioned. Out of such accounts rose, many years later, the controversy regarding the priority of the discovery of the 'antarctic mainland'. It all hinges on whether Bransfield really saw the mainland[12], which he must certainly have approached very closely, within easy sighting distance; some historians have disparaged the claims made for Bransfield in favour of those for Palmer. It is rather curious that the same chroniclers support Wilkes's sightings, which by the same standards cannot be sustained. The Palmer arguments are all interesting but rather trivial when set

against the great circumnavigatory voyages which dared ice so much further south.

Bellingshausen, in his *Mirni* and *Vostok* (both names given in his honour to Russian IGY antarctic bases[13]), made a splendid encircling voyage with the express purpose of supplementing the discoveries of Cook. He left South Georgia early in 1820 and a year later, towards the end of his polar circumnavigation, he sighted the first land definitely to be observed within the Antarctic Circle—two islands, including Alexander I Land, only separated from the Antarctic Peninsula by a strait (now George VI Sound), thirty-two kilometres wide, of perennial ice-shelf (floating ice of immense thickness).

James Weddell, a retired British naval officer of spirit, has the distinction of being the first to get further south than Cook. After sealing in the South Orkneys (discovered by the Americans Powell and Palmer in 1821), he was enabled by unusually 'open' conditions to sail south in the sea which now bears his name to within approx. fifteen hundred kilometres of the pole, reaching lat. 74° 15′S. in long. 34° 17′W. on 22 February 1823.

The stalwart firm of Samuel Enderby and Sons, adventurous London shipowners, merchants, sealers, whalers and carriers upon the high seas, had commenced operations in 1785. Many of the most significant discoveries in antarctic seas were made by Enderby men, who were enjoined never to lose any opportunity of adding to Britain's maritime discoveries and renown. John Biscoe who circumnavigated Antarctica, annexed Graham Land[14] for Britain and amongst other discoveries, named Enderby Land during his voyage of 1831–32, has already been mentioned. He sailed through no less than fifty degrees of longitude inside the Antarctic Circle—at least nineteen hundred kilometres—in the brig *Tula*, accompanied by the 50 tonne cutter *Lively*. Kemp, a master mariner in the Enderbys' service, had his name added to the map east of Enderby Land for his discoveries in 1833. It is of interest that

James Clark Ross (Alexander Turnbull Library).

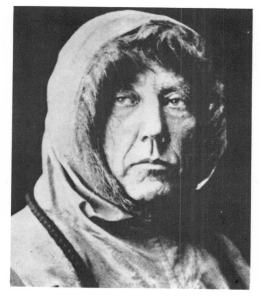

Roald Amundsen

22

it was the Enderbys' fleet of whalers which not only was the first to round Cape Horn and open up much of the Southern Ocean to the enterprise of fur- and oil-seeking but also transported many convicts to Botany Bay.

Some of the vessels used by these sealer-explorers were far smaller even than those of Cook. In 1838 John Balleny sailed for the Enderbys in a schooner, the *Eliza Scott*, of 154 tonnes, with the cutter *Sabrina*, 54 tonnes, in attendance; he eventually nudged the pack for his fifty degrees of longitude from almost directly south of New Zealand (178°E.) to a point about in line with Esperance, Western Australia. His furthest south was 69° at long. 170°E.; then he was forced north-west and beyond the Circle. He made a landing at the ice-sheathed Balleny Islands (163°E) in 1839, a venture that may have been repeated only twice or thrice since.[15] He later saw what seemed land in about 121°E. This

Antarctic leaders: Douglas Mawson and Ernest Shackleton in London, before Mawson's departure on the Australasian Antarctic Expedition, 1911–14.

Captain Scott in his sanctum, at Cape Evans, 1911. (H. G. Ponting, B.A.E., 1910–13)

was subsequently called Sabrina Land[16] by Charles Enderby in honour of the gallant little cutter which was lost in a storm with all hands.

Several other important national expeditions were undertaken during the first half of the nineteenth century. Wilkes I have already mentioned; he made two distinguished voyages—through the South Shetlands in 1839, and for about 2 400 kilometres somewhere off the coasts of the Australian sector of Antarctica in 1840. His little fleet was unsuitable, his crews disaffected, his season harsh and his resulting work inaccurate, but Dr Hugh Mill's assessment of more than seventy years ago seems likely to stand: 'Considering the deplorable conditions against which he had to contend both in the seas without and the men within his ships, the voyage of Wilkes was one of the finest pieces of determined effort on record.' His contemporaries were two of the world's most distinguished explorers: Captain Jules Dumont d'Urville of the French navy, who had already made two fine voyages round the world and carried out valuable scientific work in biology, and Captain James Clark Ross, with years of arctic voyaging behind him, including the attainment of the North Magnetic Pole in 1831.

Dumont D'Urville, in command of the *Astrolabe*,[17] had voyaged to Australia and the Pacific Islands, 1827–28, while seeking news of La Pérouse who had disappeared without trace after leaving Botany Bay, New South Wales, in 1788. In 1838 he tried, for his country's honour, to go further south than James Weddell had done fifteen years before, but he was blocked by the incalculable pack while still north of the Circle. Having fulfilled his commission as far as seemed humanly possible, and for good measure named part of the Antarctic Peninsula for his king, Louis Philippe, he rather gladly left antarctic waters. But about two years later, while in Australia, d'Urville heard of the movements of Wilkes and Ross and made a dash south to forestall them, if it should be possible, at the South Magnetic Pole. (This was, actually, to remain unvisited that century.) It was on this voyage, on 21 January 1840, that the Frenchman sighted the coast of the now-famous French sector, Adélie Land (named after Mme Dumont d'Urville). In a grey fog of misunderstanding no less than of weather d'Urville's *Astrolabe* and one of poor Wilkes's vessels, the *Porpoise*, passed each other a week later without ceremony. The record of the Frenchman's polar voyages was published after his untimely death in a railway accident. Its numerous volumes were titled, a trifle imaginatively, *Voyage au Pole Sud*.

If there is one man in the whole history of antarctic exploration who can stand beside Captain Cook, it is Ross. He had heard of d'Urville's work and had received a letter claiming extensive discoveries from Lieutenant Charles Wilkes. He was obviously piqued (although at the time he accorded Wilkes great credit), and he resolved to take an entirely different meridian to the south. This is where good fortune commenced a partnership with fine seamanship and great courage.

Shackleton's historic hut (1908–09) at Cape Royds, Ross Island.

The chosen line—170°E., where Balleny found conditions best—is, to this day, the route which may lead a ship further south than any other. When the dauntless Roald Amundsen and his party set off on their triumphant journey to the South Pole, seventy years later, they left from almost the precise point of the furthest south of James Ross, and of all Admiral Byrd's 'Little Americas' of subsequent decades.[18]

The *Erebus*, 370 tonnes, under Captain Ross, and the *Terror*, 340 tonnes, commanded by Francis Crozier, were heavily built wooden men-o'-war, wallowing vessels but very stout and strengthened for ice like the northern whalers. They reached the edge of the pack ice on the last day of 1840. There it lay in great and small floes to the southward, with immense mysterious icebergs of unknown origin standing in majesty and menace here and there, and even rising from hidden ice-strewn seas beyond the horizon. It was a sight, however expected, of a phenomenon which had foiled or intimidated all men who had ever seen it. Sometimes it had lain infinitely tranquil, a sight beyond this world, gleaming dazzlingly, seeming too vast and level to be material but perhaps with dark pools and lanes to snatch the imagination of the watcher back to his unpredictable sea. Or, again, it had heaved sullenly and dangerously, and men faced a terrible transition from the open sea, however fearful, to the grinding edge of the unknown, jagged mills of ice in which any ship of that day risked destruction.

And, of course, it is still there beyond the outriding icebergs, and the first sight of it must always astonish and awe men. I have never seen anything like it when it is calm unless it be the upper surface of a sea of sunlit

The high, still active Mount Erebus volcano forms a background to the hut built by Captain Scott at Cape Evans, Ross Island. From this hut he left on his journey to the South Pole, from which he and his companions did not return alive. The hut was built in 1910.

Beyond Shackleton's hut, at Cape Royds, Ross Island, the Ross Ice Shelf stretches 100 kilometres to the Transantarctic Mountains in the west.

clouds looked down on from a high mountain or a plane; but that is not quite right, for each of the cloud flock would need to be a cubic sheep and the upthrusting cumuli would have to be blocked in icy steps and pediments. When the edge of the pack is stormy, it is still a grey appalling nightmare. Seeing the real pack ice from the air, however, is quite different. Though lanes of open water may be visible, and the general disposition of movement apparent, the surface below seems flat, the icebergs without menace.

Five days after reaching the edge of the southern pack ice Ross and Crozier intentionally turned their vessels into it, a venture never previously undertaken. There was nothing to denote the limits of the ice-littered sea and, even in the light of his arctic experience, here was a course that demanded of Ross superlative courage and confidence. It was all brilliantly successful, for, on 10 January, the ships entered open water beyond the pack. Today the existence of this phenomenon, caused by the northerly drift in summer of the remnants of the previous year's frozen sea, is a calculated probability, but in Ross's day it could not have been foreseen. So this courageous and fortunate man sailed on towards his goal, the South Magnetic Pole.

Next day, however, an immense range of high mountains, trending south, grew strong on the horizon; it was the first indisputable landscape of Antarctica ever to be seen, and its splendour of alternating summit cliffs and glaciers has never been rivalled. Having

Memorial to Admiral Byrd, US antarctic explorer, at the McMurdo Sound Research Station, Ross Island. Byrd, having flown over the North Pole in 1926, flew across the South Pole in 1929; its first visitor since Robert Falcon Scott.

On the Ross Ice Shelf.

Training run. [D.L.]

25

named the Admiralty Range (its peaks were called after his naval masters) and Cape Adare, Ross continued gaining latitude, beyond any previously attained, and sighting new features along the western boundaries of his great new sea. The culminating discoveries occurred on 28 January 1841, when the explorers were confronted by a high ice-clad volcano in eruption and also found their course blocked by a huge barrier cliff of ice abutting the coast and stretching beyond the great volcano and its satellite cones eastward beyond sight. Ross had made a couple of token landings on off-shore islands as he followed the mountains southward from the point he named Cape Adare, but the mainland had offered nothing, every approach being hopelessly ice-filled.

Truly the nature of Antarctica was being revealed at a pace never again to be matched by subsequent explorers. Ross had penetrated the pack, a feat not dared before, with the power and the hazard of the wind alone. He proved that, with good fortune, courage and persistence in the right season, the floating ice might be negotiable and, though it take weeks to contest, could be backed by open water against the coast. A range of mountains and immense glaciers of continental proportions—a scene of 'grandeur and magnificence'—had been discovered; a volcano belching black and lurid smoke towered before them (surely no more unexpected sight was conceivable), and 'The Great Barrier', a wall of ice rising far above the masthead stretched for hundreds of kilometres to the east. Every man who has followed, appreciating the magnitude of Ross's achievements must experience vicariously something of his delight and humility. Briefly in 1965 I camped on the 'barrier' with a Russian glaciologist when much of what Ross and Crozier (and their company of 140 men) saw shone as through their description of a century and a quarter before. I know of no finer antarctic panorama.

Yet Ross was frustrated, for he had been encouraged to hope that he might sail beyond the eightieth parallel. The abrupt wall that sealed off the unknown he likened to the familiar but equally uncompromising cliffs of

Admiral Richard Byrd (1888–1957), leader of many USA expeditions.

Sir Hubert Wilkins (1888–1958), pioneer of polar aviation. [A.C.-D.]

Antarctic pioneers: Left to right: Sir Douglas Mawson, Sir Raymond Priestley and Captain John King Davis. [A.C.-D.]

Glacier crossing, Heard Island.

Dover. He called the astonishing volcano, which is on Ross Island, an interruption to the continuity of the ice-shelf or 'barrier', Mount Erebus; it remains unmatched on the antarctic continent.[19] There was no further way to be made south, so Ross steered fearlessly east, following the appalling ice cliffs for four hundred kilometres and establishing that the vast mass of ice was afloat in water hundreds of metres deep. He then returned to Hobart for the winter, not without another attempt to reach the area of the South Magnetic Pole. He also attempted to find Wilkes's landfalls but actually sailed over positions charted by the American as high land.[20] Captain James Clark Ross's 'barrier' edge was in fact the boundary of an iceberg as large as France, permanently covering half of the great gulf of the sea that bears his name. It is now known as the Ross Ice Shelf; it was a fundamental feature of Antarctica; its formation will be discussed later.

It was typical of James Ross that he returned to his enigma in the following summer, but this time, having left the Bay of Islands in New Zealand, he sailed for the pack on a course much further east. As subsequent exploration has revealed, he met the ice-floes on the edge of an area where the disposition of winds and currents and the trend of the coasts cause an accumulation which must at times occupy eight hundred thousand square kilometres of the Southern Ocean.

Frequently the first really calm water an expedition comes upon is in the pack, where the floes damp the movement of the sea. On this voyage, however, Ross experienced one of the most frightful storms in history, the huge swell bombarding the *Erebus* and *Terror* with great blocks of ice, smashing their rudders and threatening to dash the two ships together and to pieces. The seas were described by Ross as 'an ocean of rolling fragments of ice, hard as floating rocks of granite'. Yet the storm was weathered. Whether night, black and pro-

found, with ghostly spume mounting high above the wallowing ship, with the shriek of wind and the thump of unseen floes, is more or less frightening than day, visible mist and spray-filled air moaning and rattling, green seas sweeping the decks, the tops of waves severed and hurled against the bridge and the vessel leaning further than fear can countenance; whether night or day is more intimidating in a storm at sea, I cannot decide. But, at least, in our day we have radar and communication with the world, not only a voice to God. So few today travel anywhere by sea. I cannot think, though, that our present times, when almost everyone rides a projectile over the fathomless sea, have not lost some challenge (whatever dreads and problems they impose) that once strengthened the heart of man.

On his second voyage Ross entered the pack on 18 December 1841 at 60°S., 146°W. The vessels were no less than six weeks ice-encumbered, but in that time covered more than twelve hundred kilometres through the floes. At one stage the audacious Ross actually had both his vessels, under full sail, moored to a suitable floe which he used as a battering ram. Ross must stand alone for enterprise and courage in antarctic navigation. On another occasion before that voyage ended, after an unavoidable collision with the *Terror*, he backed the *Erebus* stern first in a hurricane to avoid an iceberg. He had 'the maintack hauled on board sharp aback—an expedient that perhaps had never before been resorted to by seamen in such weather'. All men who breast the ice in modern ships should read Ross and be comforted.

Ross came upon his 'barrier' three weeks after leaving the pack ice, and his eastward departure this time took him to long. 161° 27'W. in the highest latitude he attained—78° 11'S.—close to the end of the ice-shelf near King Edward VII Land (named by Captain Scott many years later). He returned to his original route of the previous year through a thickening sheet of new ice late in the season and, after other dangers well countered, eventually he reached the Falkland Islands. A third summer in the antarctic seas did not add to Ross's achievements owing to the vagaries of ice in the Weddell Sea, his chosen sector for 1843.

After Ross no one entered the open water of his sea for more than fifty years; interest in the Antarctic lapsed while the Arctic again sprang into focus on account of Sir John Franklin's tragic attempt to discover a north-west passage from the Atlantic to the Pacific, across the north of Canada.

When interest in the south again quickened it was in response not only to the age-old incentives of adventure and fame but, more than ever before, to the spur of science. From the time of James Ross to the present day (and perhaps, strange thought, since James Cook) men have lived from one expedition to the next, by word of mouth, to advise and inspire their successors and probably to give them the little personal wrinkles that have escaped all the official chronicles. Sir Joseph Banks (1744–1820) certainly knew Sir John Ross who doubtless inspired his nephew, James Clark Ross. Banks had sailed with Cook; Sir John Ross was a noted Arctic explorer. It is an extraordinary chain. One of Ross's surgeons in the Antarctic was destined to be numbered amongst the greatest scientists of his century. This was Joseph Hooker (1817–1911) who never failed to urge the importance of science to further antarctic exploration (and vice versa). It is curious to recall his narrow escape during Ross's first antarctic voyage when he fell into the sea, was nearly crushed between the landing boat and the shore of Franklin Island on 27 January 1841 and, badly chilled, was hauled on board. His voice sounded through the rest of the century. He survived to see the first great scientific expeditions of the twentieth century and had close contact with their leaders, Robert Falcon Scott and Ernest Shackleton. They, of course, advised Mawson and Davis who gladly gave assistance to many now living. I have notes from Mawson containing hints on such diverse matters as wooden toggles versus zip-fasteners, dog-harness of heavy lampwick and the labelling of rock specimens. He also spoke feelingly about the means of defecation in blizzard. That advice was certainly handed down from the first sledging parties.[21]

Before it closed, the nineteenth century witnessed three significant antarctic conquests. The first circumscribed adventure itself, for there was an element of routine brought about by the splendid nonchalance of the masters of small whaling vessels which cruised outside the pack or along the coasts of the Antarctic Peninsula. Many of these expeditions were Scandinavian, men and vessels that had felt the shock of the hard arctic floes. The old names are familiar: Larsen, Christensen, Andersen, Evensen, Petersen, Amundsen and others; many of their vessels sailed out from the

Beachmaster, Macquarie Island. The male elephant seal with, erect proboscis roars at an intruder; an expedition relief vessel is anchored in the distance.

The skyline of this large iceberg, grounded in shallow water for several seasons, reveals delicate sculpture, the result of erosion by sun and wind.

Open water beyond the pack. In summer, in many parts, the pack ice drifts north, leaving calm open water along the coast.

old ports and the fabulous fiords under the watchful eye of such vikings and veterans as old Svend Foyn. They and the adventurers of other nations—British, American, Russian, Japanese—brought close to extinction the quarries they sought and there has been a world-wide revulsion against their ruthless slaughter. Though the whalers were fundamentally interested in what the southern waters might yield, they were often experienced explorers, and they recorded and mapped their discoveries, eventually producing their own charts of the whaling coasts. Several fine polar explorers served their apprenticeship in whalers, including Dr W. S. Bruce, who sailed with a Dundee craft in 1892, and Carstens Borchgrevink, a resident of Melbourne who joined Foyn's expedition of 1894–95 under Kristensen in the *Antarctic*. This voyage was notable, for during its course the first landing on the antarctic mainland was made at Ross's Cape Adare.

The second conquest was a slender, almost Pyrrhic, victory over the midday darkness of the antarctic winter, and perhaps it was thrust upon the *Belgica's* commander and company, who nevertheless acquitted themselves more than creditably. The Belgian expedition, like several other later and larger national ventures, arose from the International Geographic Congress of 1895, held in London. It was a private scientific venture, owing its very existence to its leader, Adrien de Gerlache, who obtained a vessel of only 250 tonnes and barely sufficient equipment. Its work commenced in late 1897 in Tierra Del Fuego and continued with the taking of valuable soundings between South America and the Antarctic Peninsula.

Fast-ice still attached to the coast prevents the expedition vessel reaching the Davis station. After a few days the ice was dissipated by the powerful coastal currents.

A plume of steam floats from the summit of Mount Erebus, the active volcano, 4 023 metres high, dominating Ross Island.

The storm barrier: all expedition ships pass through the stormy forties and fifties of south latitude before reaching the relative calm of the pack ice.

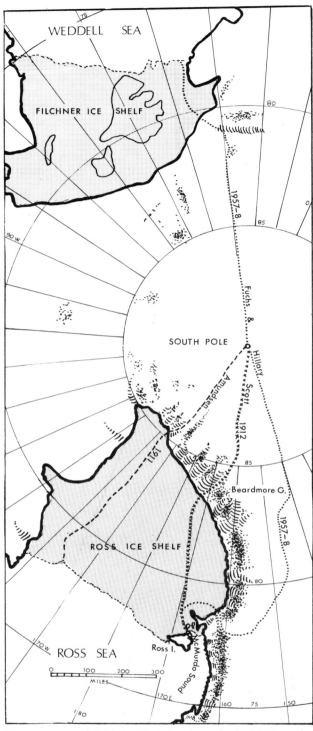

WEDDELL SEA

FILCHNER ICE SHELF

SOUTH POLE

ROSS ICE SHELF

ROSS SEA

Ross I.

The attainment of the South Pole. Amundsen's party reached the South Pole on 14 December 1911; Scott's achieved the same object only thirty-five days later, on 18 January 1912. On 29 November 1929 Richard Byrd flew over the Pole, and on 31 October 1956 Dufek and his team landed in preparation for founding a geophysical station there as an IGY project. The British leader, Fuchs, and the New Zealander, Hillary, met later at the US polar station, having pioneered routes from, respectively, the Weddell and Ross Seas. The Commonwealth Trans-Antarctic Expedition completed its crossing of Antarctica in ninety-nine days, having travelled 3 461 kilometres, and arrived at McMurdo Sound on 2 March 1958. Both USA and USSR soon after completed their surface traverses to the Pole, from Mirni (USSR) and from McMurdo Sound and Little America V (USA).

It was late in the season by the time de Gerlache had isolated the Palmer Archipelago (south of the South Shetlands) from the area of the Antarctic Peninsula known as Graham Land and he found himself beyond the seventieth parallel at the end of February. Perhaps half intentionally, half fatalistically, and certainly against the desire of most, he let the *Belgica* be driven southwards until she was beset by ice and beyond the point of any possible return that season. It was certainly much to the advantage of the cosmopolitan company on board that it included not only the quixotic commander and the brave Captain Lecointe but a clear-eyed, imperturbable Norwegian mate called Roald Amundsen and an extraordinarily resourceful American physician, Dr Frederick Cook.

No description of shortening days and the approach of winter could fully have prepared the expedition for the misery and uncertainty, the interminable storm and darkness, of the months that followed. Ill-equipped, improperly provisioned, insufficiently lit and warmed, the *Belgica* and her company entered the loneliness and gloom of the first polar winter experienced by human beings in the southern hemisphere. Everyone became emaciated and ill; Lieutenant Danco, the geomagnetician, died. Yet meteorological and other observations were recorded and ultimately were considered of great value; they were more extensive than the scientific results of any previous antarctic expedition.

Some of the dramatis personae of the drift of the *Belgica* in the Bellingshausen Sea, to almost the same latitude as Captain Cook had reached on 30 January 1774, played other parts, triumphant or tragic, in future polar events. When I was preparing for the IGY I was oddly moved; into my room at ANARE's[22] Melbourne headquarters, entered an upstanding Belgian with a special interest in the forthcoming International Geophysical Year. It was Count Gaston de Gerlache de Gomery, son of the commander of the *Belgica*.

The third special victory I mentioned came only a year after the *Belgica* had left the ice (largely owing to the resourcefulness of Frederick Cook, to whom in after years Amundsen gave unstinted credit). C. E. Borchgrevink, having obtained the necessary support of a generous patron, Sir George Newnes, found a staunch Norwegian skipper in Captain Jensen and a whaler, *The Southern Cross*, for an expedition with the object of wintering on the continent itself. After six weeks' straining against the recalcitrant pack ice in long. 165°E., a new approach more nearly in the line of Ross got them through to open water south of the ice in six hours. At Cape Adare, in mid-February 1899, Borchgrevink and his party of scientists, including L. C. Bernacchi, a Melbourne meteorologist who later sailed with Scott, set up their winter quarters. Work in geology, biology, magnetism and meteorology was undertaken and the results were of wide interest. There were no expeditions away from the coast.

So the last year of the century witnessed men in Antarctica contending with forces of gale and blizzard never previously experienced. It always takes courage to be first. Before his return in 1900 Borchgrevink followed Ross's course along the 'barrier', finding that it had receded an average of fifty kilometres. A landing on a low ice edge was made on 19 February, and a short ski journey took Borchgrevink to a point less than twelve hundred kilometres from the Pole. The national expeditions that followed in the new century had the benefit of Bernacchi's meteorological records in the Ross Sea area.

With the close of the nineteenth century there ended more than an era of time. Unprecedented powers over environment were very soon to change man's whole conceptions of his physical limitations in space and time. The great inland expeditions of the next two decades, those of Scott, Amundsen, Shackleton and Mawson, not only revealed the nature of the continent but, with the smaller but important journeys of Drygalski, Nordenskjöld, Bruce and Charcot, revealed many technical advances.

During the twentieth century the pace of exploration of all kinds has been so accelerated that more is now accomplished in a year than was formerly dreamed of in a century. It was inevitable that, in the fullness of time, man should visit every part of his planet and even its satellite moon, ranging from the upper atmosphere to space, and from the summits of all mountains to the depths of its seas, and all over its surface of desert, ocean, jungle, ice-cap, and plain. His curiosity was bound to triumph over his environment, for curiosity, even concerning the nature of danger, has always been a spur to resourcefulness. In millions of years of world history a combination of the two qualities has made man the most successful animal; only his ultimate humanity, consciousness of self, remains to dare a new quality of adventure; everything else is merely quantitative, to beyond the bounds of space.

It would be impossible and undesirable to attempt a condensation of twentieth-century antarctic exploration in this volume, for it would inevitably mean that one would never see the plateau for the ice, the great majestic ocean for the wave, or the tremendous spheres of air, the most lively element of all Antarctica, for the obscuring blizzard. The work of all modern expeditions must be synthesized for they contribute to the one great canvas, but their chronicles must not be abbreviated; these will be read whenever circumstances create sufficient desire, and I will do little more in a summary way than, as a guide, list them at the end of the book. However, as each contributes to the whole conception of Antarctica, each lives inevitably in any attempt at description. In mine is implicit experience gained as a leader of Australian expeditions, of the Antarctic Division, directed, 1949-66, by Phillip Law.

My intense feeling of contemporaneity in antarctic exploration is shared by most men who have thrust through or been beset by the pack, sledged over the infinite sastrugi or the unbroken sea-ice, and flown widely over the far south. There is little incentive to consider the twentieth century expeditions chronologically, however significant each in its own right may be. Identically the same sounds and sights and weather, the howling blizzards and the unbelievable calms, continue through them all in a truly 'timeless land'; other reasons will become apparent as we proceed.

Sledge-boxes, packed ready for dog team transport.

Fur seal, Heard Island. Ever since the days of the great fur-sealing expeditions more than 150 years ago, these eared seals have been rare. They are close relatives of the coarse-haired seals of Australian waters. [A.C.-D.]

Rising in two bizarre heaps the anchor chains of the Kista Dan, *beset in heavy pressure-ice, have been laid out on the ice in order to lighten the ship's bows and allow her to take advantage of any easing in the pressure.* [F.W.E.]

Immense snow drifts cloak the coastal ice-cliffs after a major blizzard.

The discovery of the shape of Antarctica—its actual coastline—has been very gradual since its outside limits were defined by the circumnavigatory voyages. It would be a bold geographer who asserted that even now there were no details to be defined, for it is exceedingly hard to know just where massive ice-sheets cease to overlie the land and become floating 'shelves' ready to hinge and fracture into icebergs. The means of mapping exist; sufficient time has not yet been available. Very early the 'stem' of Antarctica, the mountainous Antarctic Peninsula, projecting northward towards the South American continent, was known on its western side. It is surprising to realize that the eastern coast lay uncharted until Hubert Wilkins first used an aircraft in Antarctica (1928). In the very next summer both Douglas Mawson and Hjalmar Riiser-Larsen, the Norwegian, used planes from vessels in the Indian Ocean sector and fixed many kilometres of coast. Within weeks of Wilkins's flight, Richard Byrd had planes aloft over the Ross Ice Shelf and on 29 November 1929 he flew over the Pole. They were lonely hours that these men spent in the air, before the world at large had taken to aviation even in their gentle homelands.

The two immense gulfs occupied by the Ross and Weddell Seas are like jaws biting deep into the continent. Both of them long defied penetration because of the high 'barriers' of floating ice-shelf. Here we must go back in time and see how Robert Falcon Scott and his party carried on from Ross beyond his white walls and shaped the south-west limits of the Ross Sea to 82° 17′S. (about eight hundred and fifty kilometres from the Pole).

The second skirting of the 'barrier', after its discovery

Camp on the edge of the Ross Ice Shelf, near the Daley Islands, shared by the author with Russian and US scientists. The flags of the three nations were flown to commemorate the occasion.

Massive diesel vehicles at the Russian base, Mirni, used for major inland traverses.

Movement through the pack ice leaves a clear lane of open water in a vessel's wake.

A man-hauling survey expedition leaves the Thala Dan *bound for a then-unnamed islet in Sandefjord Bay.*

Kista Dan *beset.*

by Ross, was accomplished, and, on 30 January 1902, the rock faces of the Alexandra Mountains of King Edward VII Land at its eastern extremity provided ocular evidence of land whose existence below the rising ice was already certain. After turning back Scott went up in a captive balloon, becoming, in his own words, 'the first aeronaut to make an ascent in the Antarctic Regions'. He did not see much apart from great undulations, deceptive clouds that might have betokened land, and the tiny sledge of Armitage and Bernachi (who had been at that same place with Borchgrevink), but, had he looked 'into the seeds of time', he might have seen spread before him his great reward, transcending even the bitterness of his final journey.

He would have watched open below him a great rift in the ice-shelf as huge icebergs slowly drifted away, and seen the whales disporting there when Ernest Shackleton—six future years away—bestowed the obvious name on the calm water. He would doubtless have seen, amongst Shackleton's good company, my honoured friends John King Davis and Douglas Mawson, young men with great futures. In this Bay of Whales he would have watched Roald Amundsen (of *Belgica* fame), his fine, relentless rival, setting up his base, Framheim, for his superb race to the South Pole. Amazed, he might have descried members of Shirase's Japanese expedition of 1912 and, with a light in his eye, he might have greeted his first successors in the air over the Bay of Whales as they came in to found Little America, after being towed through the pack by the mighty *Larsen*, a 17 000 tonne whaling factory ship, in December 1928. They brought with them only three little monoplanes, under Richard Byrd, already famous for his north polar flight of 1926; but how Scott would have thrilled to see them being towed by tractor and dog teams to the site of the new station; and how precisely, in naval fashion, would he have saluted Byrd, Balchen, Parker and Smith when on 15 January 1929 they skimmed past his swaying basket, airborne on wings for the first time over the Ross Sea.

Fascinated he might have watched Ellsworth and

A beautiful, grim place: the ANARE station on Heard Island.

Penetrating the storm barrier.

Hollick-Kenyon land after their great continental flight from the Antarctic Peninsula between 21 November and 5 December 1935, during which they had risen over the Sentinel Mountains 4 000 metres high. Then there would have grown before Scott's incredulous eyes, as he stared through sixty years, all of Admiral Byrd's five bases; his surface vessels and submarines, thousands of men, hundreds of buildings, his shuddering tractors and huge aircraft, already jet-assisted, screaming over the ice. And, between these mighty operations, which led to the photo-mapping of practically the whole coast of Antarctica, Scott would have watched the Bay of Whales itself—his old Balloon Bight—disappear as square kilometres of table-topped icebergs drifted away from the inexorable pressure of the Ross Ice Shelf.

After his balloon ascent Scott returned to the western end of the shelf before setting up his winter quarters. In the next spring he sledged over the floating ice along the coast of Victoria Land to his record south latitude for the expedition of 82° 17′S., reached on 30 December, 1902. He and his men made other journeys over the ice in this and the following season, including the first great probe inland, westwards, at about 78°S., for about three hundred and twenty kilometres.

There are many expeditions which should receive credit for delineating Antarctica on our maps and (praise be!) there are opportunities still to mark the tell-tale hinge crevasses where ice-shelves meet the indisputable land-based ice. We have seen something of the Ross Sea. What of the opposing gulf and the ice-shelf of the Weddell Sea? If the former is the memorial of Ross and Scott and Amundsen, the glory of the latter is shared with

Weddell by Bruce (1904), Filchner (1912) and Shackleton (1915–16). Shackleton not only had been with Scott on Scott's first expedition but, on his own account, in the summer of 1908–09, had gone to within one hundred and fifty-six kilometres of the South Pole. For his next expedition, in 1914, he planned a trans-polar journey. Amundsen and Scott had reached the South Pole on 14 December 1911 and 18 January 1912 respectively, and Scott and his companions had died during the return journey, on the Ross Ice Shelf.

Shackleton spent the first two years of the First World War ignorant of what was happening in Europe; in the Weddell Sea they were spent in one of the most gallant struggles between man and the rest of nature that has ever occurred in history, while, on the other side of Antarctica, by Mackintosh and his benighted team, depots were faithfully laid to the foot of the Beardmore Glacier down which Shackleton hoped to descend. The sum of all the movements contained triumph and disaster and such complexities that even the several volumes written by those who were there, including Shackleton's *South*, cannot entirely tell the story. The *Endurance* became icebound in the Weddell Sea in about 75°S. on 18 January 1915, near the newly discovered Caird Coast of Bruce's Coats Land and close to Filchner's Vahsel Bay.

The drift of the *Endurance*, until she was crushed and, in November 1915, swallowed by the pressure ice, the subsequent five months while the party was carried on ice-floes, the eventual launching of small boats and the gaining of Elephant Island, are part of a modern odyssey without parallel, culminating in the boat journey to South Georgia and the crossing of that island to obtain assistance. Most of Shackleton's company remained on Elephant Island with Frank Wild, living under upturned boats, until rescue came from Chile, for four and a half months. Not since October

A backward glance as the midnight sun is left behind.

Tranquillity under the midnight sun.

Sunset in heavy pack ice.

36

Big Ben, the highest point of Heard Island, 2 800 metres, shows a clear summit rising from almost perpetual cloud at lower levels.

Castle at sunset: the remnants of a great tabular iceberg.

Magga Dan *in heavy pack*.

1914—twenty-two months before—had they had news of any kind of the outside world.

Meanwhile the Ross Sea party had been beset by tragedy, danger and discomfort, and their vessel, the *Aurora*, had broken loose in a hurricane from her moorings in McMurdo Sound (at about midnight on 6 May 1915). It was 10 January 1917 before they learned on shore what had happened to the *Aurora* and her company under Captain Stenhouse. With much of the expedition's gear and supplies on board, she had drifted into the pack before a southerly blizzard and been quite unable to regain her anchorage near Cape Evans, on Ross Island.[23] Fortunately the resourcefulness and courage of Captain J. R. Stenhouse took the *Aurora* safely through the winter pack ice to New Zealand.

The *Aurora* had been purchased by Shackleton from Douglas Mawson, whose ship's captain and second-in-command, Captain John King Davis, had done remarkable work along the coasts of the Australian sector during the years 1911–14—while Mawson was conducting one of the most generally successful antarctic expeditions that had ever taken place. When the *Aurora* again sailed south in December 1916, it was under her old master, Captain Davis, with Shackleton, straight from South America, prepared to assist in any necessary land operations.

Such is the complex story of antarctic seas and coasts; it is continued whenever a vessel thrusts aside the floes, whenever an aircraft traces the edge of the pack or the ice-cliffs, or when members of a sledging party set up their instruments to find precisely where on earth they are.

Between the wars there were several antarctic ventures: Byrd in Little America; Mawson in two years of summer cruising which helped strengthen Australia's territorial claims; John Rymill in the Antarctic Peninsula; Riiser-Larsen in consolidating Norwegian territory, and so on. After the war, from 1945, there was a spontaneous revival of interest. The United Kingdom, Argentina and Chile established several bases along the Antarctic Peninsula; Australia commenced an ambitious programme in sub-antarctic and continental research and, from 1947, has maintained a number of bases of which Macquarie Island in the sub-antarctic and Mawson, on the continent, are senior; the Norwegian-British-Swedish Expedition to Queen Maud Land (1949–52) was mounted; the USA re-established bases, and all the nations co-operating in the IGY set up more or less permanent stations. Currently the USA maintain three; the USSR, seven; Australia, four; the UK, five; Argentina, six; Chile, three; and most other interested nations, at least one permanent station.

The entire continent has been mapped in varying detail and surveys of surface, the ice mass and economy,

Ice caverns in a large tabular iceberg, probably formed while it was still part of an ice shelf attached to the continental ice.

the bed-rock foundations and of off-shore continental shelves have been made. A continuing programme of geophysics and associated sciences with full international co-operation has been active for a quarter of a century, since the IGY. Amongst the ambitious inland traverses, that of the Commonwealth Trans-Antarctic Expedition, which fulfilled Shackleton's dream of crossing the continent from the Weddell to the Ross Seas, was perhaps most notable, though there have been other major journeys and logistic triumphs, especially by the USA and the USSR, including the setting up of inland stations such as Vostok, Byrd (discontinued), Siple and South Pole. New Zealand has carried out much exploration in her own sector, notably in Victoria Land; Australia has been largely responsible for the discovery and survey of the extensive Prince Charles Mountains, of the Lambert Glacier and of the Amery Ice Shelf.

In this volume it would be impossible to describe or even list the various national contributions to our understanding of Antarctica and, indeed, to world geophysics. The International Geophysical Year commenced a consolidated international programme, with astonishing co-operation; first between the top scientific institutes of the great nations, then within the specially formed co-ordinating committees such as SCAR (the Scientific Committee for Antarctic Re-

search), and, after the signing of the Antarctic Treaty, within the periodical Antarctic Treaty Consultative Meetings of the nations party to the treaty plus others since admitted.

I shall now attempt some synopses of salient aspects of Antarctica which have been revealed as a result of consolidated exploration and research. In this I shall be eclectic, often mentioning, out of context, the work of many expeditions. The definitive history of most contemporary and continuing national expeditions has not been written.

A tribute to Amundsen and Scott, and their parties, at the South Pole.

90°S

14 December 1911   18 January 1912

R. AMUNDSEN   R. F. SCOTT
O. BJAALAND   E. A. WILSON
H. HANSSEN   H. R. BOWERS
S. HASSEL   L. E. G. OATES
O. WISTING   E. EVANS

A tribute from Great Britain and Norway 1961
Presented to the U.S. Amundsen-Scott South Pole Station

The World of Ice

There is no land on earth other than Antarctica with a coastline—incidentally of about thirty-three thousand kilometres—all in the same band of latitudes. Any such area of continental size would, of course, have to surround the Pole, north or south, and the North Pole is centred in an ocean; so Antarctica is unique. Everywhere round the continent one encounters icebergs in the stormy fifties; everywhere in the circumpolar sixties one may splinter the pack ice; somewhere in the seventies of south latitude, almost all round the huge circle, one leaves the zone of melting and ablation to the northward and enters areas of eternal sub-freezing cold. Violent streams of air, hundreds of metres deep, pour down to the coast from the plateau, keeping a prevalent direction governed by slope, mountains, ice formations and other local features and the deflection to the west induced by the rotation of the earth. Frequently these 'katabatic' winds are whitened by opaque clouds of drift snow fine as dust. The major global air circulation including that of Antarctica will be discussed later. This strange continent has a pole of course from which every direction is north, so that a northerly wind blowing towards South America actually flows in the opposite direction to one drawn towards Australia. At any point on the entire continent one may experience the antarctic blizzard or an atmosphere of utter silence and calm; nowhere does the plateau ice surface visibly differ, beyond a narrow range of tones and textures, over thirteen million square kilometres. There is no other area of the world where the ordinary senses could be so thoroughly deceived—to the extent of thousands of kilometres or, for that matter, thousands of years.

One of many reasons for feeling a unity with the past and future is what amounts to a common fear and humility. I suppose it is possible to insulate oneself from this by buttresses and walls of safety; yet all explorers would desire to face a blizzard, to experience the strange shrinking of consciousness within concentric cores of lessening integration with environment that comes of being garbed and masked in white occlusion and bitter cold. And, in this process, one knows the limits and depths of thought in an eternal moment. It does not always need a storm. I have come upon a previous season's depot far out on the plateau, left by some known predecessor in common time, and found myself turning to address him. Similarly, men finding my traces on spurs of time, high and lonely in Antarctica,

Boulders of ice, Heard Island.

have forthwith dispatched radio messages to voice their companionship, though I was at home in the friendly latitudes. Anyone who has sledged through crevassed areas in a cold mist far from the sea, and seen their black depths, may march humbly with Mawson as he continues eternally his homeward journey, companionless, to Cape Denison.

We may now conveniently consider Antarctica as a whole, as it has been revealed to men sledging on foot or with dogs, moving by tractor or by any other surface vehicle, flying in aircraft, fixed wing or movable, living through dark winters and brilliant summers. If we place ourselves outside time we may telescope the years,

drawing upon the experiences of all the expeditions in any order that clarifies our vision and aids our comprehension.

Scott, Shackleton, Amundsen and Mawson and their teams are the men who revealed the nature of Antarctica. They penetrated beyond the coastal frontiers and dared hazards which, however great they may remain objectively, for them held the added primary chill of being unknown. There is no danger but that measured by human standards. Until the unknown is illumined, the quality and quantity of its perils may be imagined only and are therefore infinite. Even today there is an entirely different atmosphere about journeying in Antarctica the moment one enters untraversed territory.

In the days of the great quartet whose names I mention Antarctica was still the Unshapen Land, a more fearful prospect than that before Perseus, and the 'grey sisters' of cold, blizzard and crevasse, such as Antarctica held, had never been encountered or estimated. These men learned how they might foil weather and ice, and they recorded everything so that future explorers would never be at their disadvantage.

Along with the chronicles of Scott and Shackleton, and such classics as Apsley Cherry-Gerrard's *The Worst Journey in the World* and Herbert Ponting's *The Great White South* must be placed *The Home of the Blizzard* by Douglas Mawson who encountered conditions probably as rigorous as any ever encountered. It was basically the fine work of Sir Douglas Mawson and his teams in King George V, Adélie and Queen Mary Lands in 1911–14[24] and in further areas of discovery in 1929–31[25] that led to the creation of Australian

The iceberg.

Iceberg towers.

Antarctic Territory in 1933, when Britain granted to Australia her own well-founded claims to a vast sector, excepting the thin slice of Terre Adélie. There are other claims, based either on exploration and proclamation or on the 'sector principle' by which certain countries assume jurisdiction southward between stated longitudes to the Pole.

Relief Map of Antarctica Ice. (Much of the basic underlying rock is depressed below sea-level.)

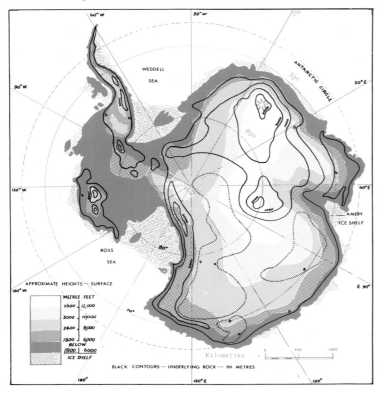

The Masson and David Ranges, in Eastern Antarctica, visible inland from the MacRobertson Land coast.

Fearn Hill, a typical coastal nunatak with a small melt-water lake at its base, in the North Masson Range, near Mawson.

Loading fuel drums in a blizzard. [P.S.]

44

Although antarctic territorial claims are implicit within the broad freedom of access granted internationally by the Antarctic Treaty, they may be evoked, especially, perhaps, to support national economic interests. If one imagines irregularly-spaced spokes as of an immense wheel, with the South Pole as axis and the sixtieth south parallel of latitude as rim, several huge sectors will be envisaged. They are British Antarctic Territory[26] (with partly coincident and overlapping claims of Chile[27] and Argentina[28]), Dronning Maud Land[29] (Norway), Australian Antarctic Territory[30], Terre Adélie[31] (France), the Ross Dependency[32] (New Zealand)—and the unclaimed Pacific sector[33].

The great inland expeditions, the shorter probes set up by various nations either on the coast or inland, and the continent's extensive aerial inspection—including that possible only by the use of satellites—have all taken place within the twentieth century. Individual ambitions and achievements have differed widely and triumphs have sometimes been blended with tragedy. Details of many operations are extraordinarily complex, yet, more and more, they contribute to the unified knowledge of the last continent.

Early in the century it became convenient among geographers to refer to East and West Antarctica because of differences that, with successive expeditions, had steadily become more obvious, the dividing line being approximately 0°–180° compound meridian of Greenwich and the International Date Line. Between the two divisions lie the great indentations of the Ross and Weddell Seas and a transcontinental lowland far below the ice linking, in its depths, the Pacific and Atlantic Oceans.

Today it may be confidently asserted that the continental ice of Antarctica is anything from 300 metres to

Wind-scour, Casey Range. Immense open pits, formed and kept open by wind, occur very often against the abrupt rock walls of mountains projecting through the antarctic ice.

A solitary vehicle passes beyond a massive wind-scour, near Mount Twintop, south of Mawson.

Exploring in the Framnes Mountains, Australian Antarctic Territory.

five kilometres thick; such determinations have formed an important part of the glaciological programmes of all nations. Methods of obtaining soundings have varied, extraordinary developments using radar having occurred in the last quarter of the twentieth century, and information relayed to earth from satellites has augmented maps revealing the under-ice contours of Antarctica. Still a standard method of obtaining depths, and valuable in checking electronically gained results, is seismic sounding where shock waves originating from explosions taking place, under controlled conditions, in drill holes near the surface, are reflected by the underlying rock and recorded by geophones spaced out in the vicinity. Time of reflection, degree of refraction and other information may be equated with depth and density of ice. Seeming anomalies in gravity, detected by sensitive gravimeters, may also be used in confirmation of variations in the main rock foundations.

Such a ponderous overburden is calculated to have depressed several areas of Antarctica below sea-level, so it is now accepted by glaciologists that the 'continent' consists of at least three land masses and some islands fused together in a great matrix of ice. Soundings over the main lobe (East Antarctica), almost entirely within longitudes east of Greenwich, show vast inland depressions below sea-level. Later I shall again refer to this extraordinary deformation and to the ice mass in general.

What is now apparent, as in a vision from space, is a colossal white mass, irregular in outline, higher than any other average continental elevation, into which Europe or the USA could fit with plenty to spare, surrounded by a vast fringe of frozen sea bearing immense table-topped icebergs.

Geological studies initiated by Edgeworth David and Raymond Priestley in 1907–09, and continued by many others, have revealed that the high mountains first sighted by Ross in 1841, walling the western side of his sea, were uplifted as a great horst between parallel faults running right across Antarctica, raising ancient strata of sediments thousands of metres thick and immense sheets or sills of volcanic rocks to heights exceeding 4 000 metres above sea-level. Isolated peaks exceeding 4 600 metres have been surveyed. Beyond these mountains, through which Shackleton and Scott toiled by way of the Beardmore Glacier, Amundsen taking the Axel Heiberg, and through which all their successors including Fuchs and Hillary have had to find passages by such glacial valleys, lay East Antarctica, a huge, laterally inflexible shield of granitic rocks against which the mountain-raising forces of the Pacific area thrust themselves.

The general theory, as promulgated by Griffith Taylor (who had been with Scott, 1910–11), would link the systems of young fold mountains of New Zealand, through those of West Antarctica and the Antarctic Peninsula, with the Andes, by way of a loop taking in South Georgia. It suggested a downfold or geosyncline, probably largely filled with ice and sagging under its enormous weight, right across Antarctica. Subsequent

The birth of an iceberg. [P.G.L.]

A field of icebergs immobilized in the frozen sea. The direction of the prevailing wind is clearly shown by the tongues of surface drift. [R.A.A.F.]

A pattern of ancient weathering on the surface of ice near the eternally frozen Beaver Lake in the Prince Charles Mountains.

work appears entirely to confirm the early brilliant hypothesis, especially when linked with modern plate tectonics and the drift of continents. The structure of Antarctica has many similarities, as Griffith Taylor suggested, with Australia, the granite shield of Western Australia and the horsts of the south-eastern highlands corresponding, respectively, to East Antarctica and the ranges of Victoria Land.

At Byrd, the American research station on the eightieth parallel, between the Ross and Weddell Seas, an ice-depth of 3 048 metres was sounded at an altitude of 1 520 metres above sea-level. Subsequent US traversing with seismic sounding apparatus revealed an astonishing continuation of such great depths of ice and, of course, of their rock foundations. Eventually it was established that the immense volume of ice discovered at Byrd filled a broad trough, averaging about six hundred kilometres in width, linking the beds of the Ross and Bellingshausen Seas. So West Antarctica gradually became an archipelago. Furthermore, newly discovered extensions of the Filchner Ice Shelf, south of the Weddell Sea, were linked to the general system of subnévéan troughs. The Antarctic Peninsula is now seen to be an island attenuated far southwards well beyond 80°S. latitude, where the seabeds of the Pacific and Atlantic Oceans join.

The hinterland of each scientific base, during the last two or three decades, has been similarly probed, using more and more sophisticated means that have enabled extensive and effective aerial traversing. In Western Antarctica the Sentinel Range of the Ellsworth Mountains, of highly folded metamorphic rocks, was found to rise close on 5 000 metres (Mt Tyree is 4 922 metres). South of the Australian base at Mawson the discovery and exploration of the Prince Charles Mountains has continued through more than twenty years since my party had the good fortune to be first-footers there. These mountains are of Pre-Cambrian igneous and metamorphic rocks with some later vulcanism, but a most significant discovery in the area has been the formerly unsuspected extension inland of the Amery Ice Shelf into which the Lambert Glacier, claimed to be the largest in the world, drains the ice-streams of the Prince Charles Mountains.

Obvious in many parts of the coast, the rock foundations of East Antarctica are granites and gneisses, schists and other ancient (Pre-Cambrian) rocks metamorphosed by pressure and heat. Overlying them, in many areas, are sediments including limestones and the coal-bearing sandstones, such as the Beacon series named by Ferrar in 1907, themselves in parts covered by later plutonic intrusions. In the coastal regions of East Antarctica the granites have been laid bare by ice action, and geologists have travelled hundreds of kilometres from the sea before discovering sedimentary rocks outcropping above the ice. This is typically so of the mountainous areas inland from the coasts of MacRobertson and Dronning Maud Lands. The Trans-

Jagged mountains and smooth drifts in the Twintop area, south of Mawson.

Rock exposures, near Mount Twintop, south of Mount Coates.

The wind-sculpted surface of the plateau over millions of square kilometres has this typical pattern of sastrugi.

antarctic Mountains containing the many ranges of the great Antarctic Horst extend from the western shores of the Ross Sea to the eastern edge of the Weddell Sea.

In West Antarctica an entirely different geological structure is apparent. There are few areas revealing Pre-Cambrian rocks and even the older fossil-bearing strata are rare, but deposits of the middle and later periods —Triassic to Pliocene—are found over wide, frequently extensively folded, mountain regions. The younger rocks are rich in fossils, providing absolute evidence of a vastly different climate in past time, with plants that bore many close resemblances to those of both temperate and tropical lands today. There has also been considerable recent volcanic activity in West Antarctica.

A fascinating theory of the origins of Antarctica, in fact of all the southern continents, was originally proposed by Eduard Suess (1831–1914), a celebrated Austrian geologist, in his great work, *The Face of the Earth*. His view, which had commanded attention for three-quarters of a century, has now been accepted by all leading geologists. Antarctica once formed part of a super-continent which Suess called Gondwanaland (after an area in central India). This vast landmass contained also South America, Africa, India and Australia. These southern continents drifted apart, their deep foundations in the semi-fluid magma of a substratum of the earth's crust. It has never been difficult, of course, to rearrange in imagination the huge fragments of the mighty jig-saw puzzle—the continents as we know them—into a plausible whole. Western Africa so nearly accommodates eastern South America, and India

Mountains of Oates Land, photographed during a flight from McMurdo Sound to New Zealand.

Transantarctic Range which divides East from West Antarctica, viewed during a flight to the South Pole.

and Australia, with a small fill-in from Madagascar, may be neatly contiguous with Antarctica. However, absolute proof of the correctness of Suess's theory came in stages. Various geosynclines, great structural down-folds, coal measures and glacial deposits could be matched if the continents were rearranged as seemed logical; rock formations corresponded well enough; the final proof resulted from accurate assessment of disruptive movements by the matching of ancient magnetic alignments 'imprinted' in the texture of rocks while they were still being formed; this made the former contiguity of rocks absolutely certain.

Since the central premise was accepted the theory of 'Plate Tectonics'[34] now seeks to clarify the reasons why the continents drifted, and continue to drift, apart. It presumes the continents part of rigid crustal 'plates' moving, over-riding and hinging in mid-oceanic depths where upwelling magmas thrust the plates further apart and probably compensate for the depression of the ocean beds by the colossal weight of sediments eroded from the land. The incidence of volcanic and seismic activity in any part of the world is inversely proportional to its distance from the juncture of plates. Attempts have also been made to extend to both hemispheres the consolidated land area of the Jurassic Period[35] when the continents probably began to separate: the last points of contact over immense periods providing bridges for flora and fauna and the links that still exist between evolving families and genera. This theory of Alfred Wegener, the German explorer, set forth in his *Origin of Continents and Oceans*, has also gained acceptance. The drift of continents certainly explains great climatic change, as evident in fossil remains in frigid countries of plants and animals that required temperate or tropical conditions for their growth and existence.

The one illimitable element is time, and time adds credence to changes otherwise inconceivable. Movements of the order of two or three centimetres a year, almost imperceptible in the human scale, would raise altitudes twice as high as Everest in less than a million years. That movements do occur, especially in levels of ice and sea, may be seen in many parts of the coast of Antarctica where wave-cut terraces have risen, relative to our present sea-level, by several metres.

During his arctic voyage of 1610–11 Henry Hudson made a distinctive cut in the rock where it rose out of the ice of the bay named after him. That mark has risen at an average rate of almost six centimetres annually during the last three hundred years because of the slow decrease in the burden of ice resting on the north of Canada. There is no doubt that in Antarctica, too, the ice-level has fallen considerably, in some areas by a hundred or more metres. On the summits of coastal mountains near Mawson I have seen glacial erratics —boulders moved from far away to their present positions by the agency of ice—deposited up to two hundred metres above the level of the existing ice-sheet. Rise in sea-level caused by the melting of ice, though this may be modified by changes in ocean floors or land-levels, is, generally speaking, world-wide and has been

A much eroded iceberg. [G.W.]

A view taken from a summit in the David Range. The peaks may be distinguished in the aerial view of the coast.

Antarctica. The arrow indicates the site of Mawson station on Horseshoe Harbour. In the background are the Masson and David Ranges projecting from ice a thousand metres thick.

estimated at 1.2 millimetres annually during the first half of the twentieth century.[36] Obviously the interaction of many diverse factors provides a complex resultant.

We may state with certainty, from the evidence of fossil plants, including the thick seams of coal occurring over thousands of kilometres in the Transantarctic Mountains, that ice overwhelmed a formerly fertile continent. It is today presumed that the drift of continents is the main explanation. Antarctica, it would seem, must have been edged into the polar regions, displacing other landmasses now temperate or tropical which certainly show evidence of past glaciation in ice-scored rocks and U-shaped valleys. There is recent evidence of ancient glaciation in Antarctica itself, tillites laid down before the coal which is of Permian period, and the great quantities of fossil sub-tropical plants, of Jurassic period, existing in West Antarctica.[37]

One may imagine how, in the slow passage of time, gradually, the snows of winter ceased to melt on the mountains; how they crept down the slopes and at length lay through the summers even in the valleys. Then, by degrees, many mammals and other animals must, with plant life, have perished or adapted themselves to the infinitely slow changes. This evolution in time is very difficult for our minds to comprehend. We must estimate what seems a long period in our history, say, since Julius Caesar landed in Britain—two thousand years—as a brief instant in geological time. Inexorably, if our theory is correct, all life must have migrated towards the coasts and ultimately taken to the sea, seals and penguins evolving limbs from legs and wings used by their land and air ancestors to swim and fly through water. It is again almost inconceivable that sufficient favourable mutations could have occurred to make this possible. It might help to think that, since Jurassic times, man could have evolved from his hominid ancestors fifteen or twenty times over. The very first mammals may have begun their evolution at about the same time as the beginning of the great continental drift.

Then the frozen deposits of successive centuries must finally have filled the valleys and overtopped the mountains, becoming more and more compressed under their own weight until they became solid ice. Such ice is formed by a slow continuous process as the air is forced to the surface; in the constantly sub-freezing climate of the antarctic plateau—where there is virtually no surface melting such as occurs in the snowfields of gentler latitudes, causing water to percolate through the drifts —always a certain amount of air remains trapped and compressed. A quantitative estimation of this and of the degree of its compression leads to a reckoning of the age of the ice samples. Dating is also possible by analysing the air content of the bubbles for isotopes of carbon

51

and oxygen. Over a period of years the average annual increment of crystalline snow or *névé* may be measured against stakes planted in selected areas. As a rule it amounts to a few centimetres only, less than the precipitation recorded in many of the world's most arid deserts. Dry and non-adhesive because of the intense cold, much of the antarctic snow is blown northward out to sea, or until it forms lee drifts in mountainous regions. How bleak many of those inland mountains are, black and bleak and too cold for dry snow to adhere! Sometimes, in the walls of a pit dug in the *névé*, it is possible to discern faint seasonal striae where the finer weather of summer, when there is little precipitation but an almost daily movement of scurrying drift, polishes a surface buried in subsequent darker days. Innumerable drilled ice-cores obtained all over Antarctica by present-day geologists, refrigerated, and kept so until they are fully analysed in distant overseas laboratories, tell the same story.

So, on the plateau, one may pass down through history, penetrating snows that fell in former years, in distant centuries. A core lifted by an ice-drill may bring to the eye the precipitation of the year that Captain Cook circumnavigated the pack ice and commenced our history of the far south. You could melt ice-crystals for your evening drink that had lain frozen since the time of Christ. The yearly 'horizons' revealed in cross-sections of the ice receive considerable quantities of meteoric and volcanic dust, of radioactive particles from nuclear explosions, of pollen, of airborne bacteria

and of other evidence of what happens in the atmosphere of our planet. Correlated with the dating of samples such evidence monitors many world events, including volcanic eruptions, atomic fallouts, and such insidious changes as are caused by the increased use of leaded petroleum fuels. One recent ice-depthing south

Crevassing and melt-water channels in coastal ice-slopes. Such 'ablation' zones occur mainly within a few kilometres of the sea.

Aerial view of typical antarctic coastal cliffs of ice rising thirty or more metres from the sea-ice, and floating six times as deep. An iceberg has detached itself; it will float northward when the summer breaks up the fast-ice.

Glacier tongue, Ross Sea, flowing from the mountains of Victoria Land, north of McMurdo Sound.

Frozen spray at the coast, as temperatures fall and the sea begins to freeze.

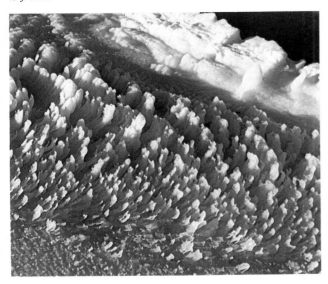

Descent into a crevasse. [K.G.]

of Casey revealed that the bedrock lay 4.8 kilometres below. That is a great deal of history!

Starting with the Norwegian-British-Swedish Expedition to Dronning Maud Land (1949–52)—the first of the post-war scientific ventures in the still continuing concentration of international interest, seismic, gravitational and radar methods of ice-depthing have been used over most parts of Antarctica to reveal the topography of the land beneath the ice. Extraordinary and unexpected variations were found, proving that whole mountain ranges and depressions far below sea-level lay beneath the ice. The Americans proved that even the South Pole, long thought to be high because of underlying rock, actually must be produced downwards through something over 2.7 kilometres of *névé* and ice to stand on a rock base. There have been innumerable traverses: a Russian seismic programme, in five hundred kilometres south of Mirni at no place sounded bedrock above sea-level; French scientists dis-

covered depressions in Adélie Land six hundred metres below sea-level; an Australian expedition southward along the sixty-second meridian showed ice-depths of 2.5 kilometres and several mountain ranges that were completely buried. In any summer now, radar depthing flights may cover ten thousand kilometres.

Even before it was firmly established that there had been considerable downward displacement of the earth's crust below the antarctic ice it was reckoned that the quantity of water immobilized in the continent today could raise the levels of all oceans by seventy-five metres, drowning many of the world's greatest cities. More recent estimates, because of the presumed consequent land-level changes, have been decreased to about forty metres. However, such a rise would be extremely discomforting, with only the tallest buildings in London and New York, for instance, islanded by the sea. It is fortunate that such changes appear to take place

53

Frost-plastered ridge, Heard Island. Such deposition does not occur further south on the antarctic continent where temperatures are too low to allow dry blown snow to adhere to rock.

A lull in the weather during an attempt to climb Big Ben, Heard Island.

over periods measurable only in terms of geological time.

The surface of the planet would present a very different appearance, coastlines would be much longer, and many ancient land bridges would still exist were it not for the plasticity of ice under pressure. Because of this the central ice mass expands laterally as well as depressing the rock beneath. The gravitational force in effect causes radial coastal movements over all Antarctica, and when the ice-sheets overflow the edge of the land and float on the sea they form ice-shelves and, as they become detached, tabular icebergs. Frequently, especially from the air, immense crevassed glaciers are seen, vast slow-moving streams which, on the surface, would be scarcely comprehensible as such. When mountains deflect the flow it is often possible to see patterns in unusual moraines of rock fragments carried on the surface. Far inland, where the cold is most intense and where ablation's effect must exceed that of gravity, and where surface movement is slow, small pieces of rock may remain on a wind-polished surface near mountains for countless years; but in coastal regions, where surface melting takes place in summer and where stones absorb and hold more radiant heat from the sun, the smaller fragments sink below the surface and, at a distance from the peaks, only the great monoliths remain above the ice moving seawards, in an extraordinary linear procession. The rate of movement of ice varies, of course, with slope, distance from the sea, depth, nature of the underlying terrain, and temperature. Diagrams showing 'particle paths' from the time snow crystals are absorbed at the surface, at various distances inland, until they reach virtual bedrock have been compiled and, as has been mentioned, the time involved may be in the order of 200 000 years.[38] As the particles sink, most vertically far inland where lateral

ice movement is slight, they are also advancing coastwards where they are eventually extruded in the base of icebergs breaking away from ice-cliffs or shelves.

Surface movements may be measured by taking a series of sights periodically with a theodolite between a mark set up on the ice and some fixed outcrop, a mountain peak or a nunatak.[39] The Ross Ice Shelf appears to be being pushed northward at the rate of more than a metre a day at its 'barrier' edge. Plateau ice 600 metres above the MacRobertson Land coast was estimated to be advancing, on the average, only three centimetres daily. At this rate, rocks falling from mountains fifteen kilometres south of Mawson would take more than a thousand years to reach their inevitable destination at the edge of the sea.

Today, just as methods of measuring ice-depths by radar have almost superseded the older seismic techniques, which, however, are used where necessary in confirmation of seeming anomalies, satellites and electronics are now used for the measurement of ice movements. Radio receivers on the ice surface record precisely on tape the pitch of a signal from a satellite passing overhead, the position of which is constantly known. The change in pitch as the satellite approaches and recedes[40] enables the exact location of the survey receiver set and its accompanying stake, firmly driven into the *névé*, to be calculated. Further observations at planned intervals, usually of two or more years, reveal the new positions of stakes and, consequently, the speed and direction of surface ice movements. The satellite technique is used for key stakes fifty or more kilometres apart; the positions of intermediate stakes may be obtained by surface surveying, using theodolites for angles and directions and a tellurometer[41] for linear measurements.

Were it not that the icebergs calved from the polar glaciers and ice-fronts complete the great water-cycle and eventually replenish the surrounding oceans, these oceans would by now probably be disconnected seas, and the whole balance of the earth would be disturbed!

It should be noted, as is quickly brought to the notice of the antarctic traveller, that, although ice is plastic in its behaviour under great pressure, it is not fluid, and it may be too brittle not to fracture in conforming to the stresses imposed upon it by gravity and the underlying rock or the deflecting pinnacles of mountains that stand above its surface. The cracks and fissures so caused may vary in width from almost nothing up to dozens of metres and their depths may range to fifty or sixty metres, an absolute limit probably being reached where the pressure overcomes the ice's hardness and resistance to deformation. These cracks or crevasses make travelling on the surface difficult and, if they are covered by thin superficial layers of snow or *névé*, dangerous.

Men of all expeditions exploring the plateau become familiar with and wary of crevasses. Near the coast they are often very common owing to the close gravitational pull of the ice-cliffs, but they are then generally more easily visible, since they occur in the area of ablation, where surface snow is either blown off the old basic blue ice that has moved north from far inland, or

melted away under the strong summer sun and by the ameliorating effect of relatively warm open water and rock exposures close at hand. The coastal ablation zone[42] varies with season and latitude, of course, but as a rule, not many kilometres inland upon the plateau, which generally rises steeply to some thousands of metres, one reaches its apparent limits. Farther south, always, the air and ice temperatures are well below the freezing point of water, and even the radiant heat of the sun cannot visibly affect the surface. On the white *névé*, naturally, most of the light and heat is reflected back into the atmosphere and not absorbed; even where dark mountains project, well inland, rock temperatures, affected by radiant heat or the ambient air, still remain below freezing and no wastage by melting takes place.[43]

Crevasses are generally bridged wholly or partly by drift snow and *névé*. There is frequently a visible difference of texture between the bridge and its margins and often a variation in tone, the bridge being lighter in colour (especially in coastal regions). A further clue to the presence of crevasses, quite common in warmer climates, is a slumping or dipping of the bridges, which become stronger in their lower central mass than at the sides, owing to progressive subsidence and consequent filling by blown drift. For this reason, the edges, where a direct break through is likely, are avoided if possible by travellers.

The snowy world of Heard Island. In one of the world's roughest climates, Heard Island lies in a zone of exceptionally heavy snowfall. Dangerous crevassing and avalanching characterize the upper slopes of Big Ben's 2 800 metre summit.

Spring sunshine on wind-polished pressure ice at coastal tide-cracks.

Opalescent effect of coastal pressure ice lit by a low sun.

Polished pressure ice on the coast.

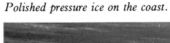

Late sunlight reveals major crevassing pattern on the antarctic plateau.

At all times, naturally, the weights of men and vehicles are distributed as widely as possible. Men travel on skis and roped together, or on sledges and vehicles with caterpillar tracks. Dogs, where they are still used, are harnessed in 'fan' formation, so that if one should break through he will not pull the others in after him. Although a few dogs remain in Antarctica, they are used mainly for recreational journeys. With few exceptions vehicles, such as 'sno-cats', 'skidoos', 'Mole Minks', tractors of varying power for hauling sledge caravans and sledge-trains, and the formerly common 'weasels', do not press as heavily over a unit area as the human foot, so, provided that the crevasse bridge *as a whole* stands, the passage of a heavy vehicle or sledge may be considerably safer than the crossing of a man on foot. This fact was demonstrated memorably enough for me when, properly roped, I was leading a reconnaissance in heavily crevassed snow previously traversed in safety, high on a glacier in Heard Island. The interval between carefully probing my way forward, and dangling at the end of a six metre nylon rope, was imperceptible. Fortunately, the rope had bitten deep into part of the snow bridge behind me—I had unconsciously been moving almost parallel with a crevasse—and had cushioned my descent into the abyss which passed rapidly through tones of exquisite blue to the black depths. Fortunately, too, my ice-axe was held by its wrist loop and, although one glove had been torn from its harness, I had a spare which I could reach while slowly twisting between the ice walls. My second on the rope had also broken the bridge but had not dropped far and was able to climb out. Eventually, well anchored, my companions, Shaw and Elliott, were able to lower me a second rope with a 'stirrup', so making an ascent easy.

A tragic crevasse accident occurred on 14 December 1912, during Douglas Mawson's great dog-sledging

Dawn in the Vestfold Hills, close to Davis station.

Floe reflections. In pack ice, because of the damping effect of the floes, the sea is often mirror smooth.

journey across King George V Land, between Adélie Land and Ross's Admiralty Range. Lieutenant B. E. S. Ninnis was travelling behind Mawson and Dr Xavier Mertz, with his sledge and dogs. Mawson and Mertz rode their sledge over *névé* in which were the very faint indications of crevassing. Ninnis walked by his sledge, although he turned his team to cross the area at right angles—the safest way. He and his team and sledge suddenly broke through and disappeared forever.

Mawson wrote: 'It was but one of many hundred similar ones we had crossed and had no specially dangerous appearance . . . The explanation appeared to be that Ninnis had walked by the side of his sledge, whereas I had crossed it sitting on the sledge. The whole weight of a man's body bearing on his foot is a formidable load and no doubt was sufficient to smash the arch of the roof.'

Crevassing is, on the whole, much more static in Antarctica than it is in its better-known occurrence on steep mountain glaciers, but it follows a similar kind of time sequence, infinitely retarded. As the ice moves beyond the cause of its fracture, the surface gradually heals, but further crevasses open behind it in the same region relative to the cause.

It should now be possible to visualize Antarctica as, basically, a vast lobe[44] of high undulating rock lying mainly in eastern longitudes fronting Africa, the Indian Ocean and Australia, and, in western longitudes, facing the Pacific Ocean, two large islands and several smaller ones between the Ross and Weddell Seas. Both regions are united by colossal masses of ice, some five kilometres deep, often over-topping mountains and falling to depths in depressions of the earth's crust far below sea-level. Under gravity—its own tremendous weight and pressure—this continental ice is plastic and spreads in slow constant movement, over-riding the land into the sea which it fronts as high cliffs continually spawning immense icebergs, or on which it floats

The Lambert Glacier that flows down from the Prince Charles Mountains to the Amery Ice Shelf, said to be the longest glacier in the world. [R.R.]

as shelf-ice still attached to that on land, three hundred or more metres thick. The edges of ice shelves, such as those covering much of the Ross and Weddell Seas, present formidable barriers from which are detached by far the largest icebergs in the world. Ice shelves usually cover enclosed bays and gulfs and are nourished by immense glaciers channelling the plateau ice through gaps in high mountains by which otherwise it is constrained. The glaciers of the Transantarctic Mountains and of the Ellsworth Mountains at the head of the Antarctic Peninsula feed the Ross and Filchner Ice Shelves; the newly surveyed Amery Ice Shelf, in the Indian Ocean sector, by the Lambert Glacier, claimed to be the largest in the world, conjoining the ice-streams of the Prince Charles Mountains. Including its ice

The crater of Mount Erebus, the still active volcano on Ross Island. [US NAVY]

Icefall of glacier on Mount Erebus, Ross Island. [US NAVY]

shelves the area of Antarctica may be extended to perhaps 14 000 000 square kilometres. Over all this ice, as we have seen, whenever its smooth flow is interrupted —by underlying rock, by a change of gradient, by mountains or the close proximity of sea—there are areas of tension where crevassing may occur.

Surrounding Antarctica the sea carries immense quantities of land-formed ice, returned, after millennia, to oceanic circulation; it also itself freezes over for many months of the year for distances up to three hundred or so kilometres off-shore, above a continental shelf depressed to a depth two or three times that of other continental shelves. Incidentally, it will be realized that when the sea freezes the ice-sheet thickens from below. Ultimately the ice itself becomes insulation for the warmer water beneath, and so the sheet attains a maximum thickness.[45] When the ice is loosened and becomes pack ice, it may extend a thousand kilometres off-shore, with more or less widespread floes two or three metres thick.

We shall now consider a different set of elements, and some of the reasons for the existence of an ice-age in a once fertile continent. The most recent phases of its exploration reveal Antarctica not only as an ideal laboratory for studying many aspects of our planet in its solar system, but as a major influence in its weather.

The Polar Environment

So far, we have chiefly considered those aspects of Antarctica which, in man's chronology, change very slowly. Now we must think of the seasonal and cyclic changes that are so pronounced in the polar regions, and the elements of the storms and calms that still defy complete analysis and prediction. The less predictable factors of any environment are the ones that constitute its dangers for man and even beast; they also provide many of the most profitable fields for scientific study by offering the widest range of facets of any particular phenomenon. Frequently, too, they appeal to man's senses as being most impressive and memorable.

One of the most extraordinary contrasts to be discovered over the whole surface of our globe is the difference between the polar regions of the two hemispheres. The North Pole centres a great sea almost completely surrounded by continents. It will be noticed that the most continuous land latitude of all is close to the Arctic Circle,[46] running through Iceland, Norway, Siberia, Alaska, northern Canada and Greenland. The South Pole, on the contrary, even in summer, is fifteen hundred kilometres from the nearest open ocean, and the Antarctic Circle[46] is surrounded by the only continuous oceanic latitudes in the world. Here all the great oceans commingle in circumpolar loneliness, their monotony broken only by disintegrating icebergs and a few desolate islands. New Zealand is two thousand kilometres from Antarctica; Australia, three thousand five hundred kilometres, and South Africa, four thousand kilometres distant, and even Cape Horn, the

Ice break-up. [P.L.]

extremity of the nearest continent of all, is still six hundred and fifty kilometres from the attenuated tip of the Antarctic Peninsula. The great average altitude of Antarctica, approaching two thousand metres, stresses another point of contrast between the two regions, for the Arctic occupies a basin with sea-ice constantly in movement and seldom exceeding a thickness of five metres, usually much less. Fridtjof Nansen and Otto Sverdrup, 1893–96, proved, by the drift of the *Fram*,[47] that the arctic ice circulates with under-flowing ocean currents, and subsequent investigation has revealed transpolar flows ultimately entering the Atlantic by the east coasts of Greenland and Labrador. The circulation of the land-based antarctic ice is tens of thousands of times slower. It is true, of course, that Greenland possesses an ice-cap capable of calving large icebergs, but this is about one-eighth the size of that of the Antarctic.[48]

Yet, in spite of such differences, the earth's polar latitudes have many common qualities, being both equidistant, and as far as possible from the tropics. Only within the tropics is the noon sun ever directly overhead, at the zenith; at all other places on earth, the noon sun is always at an angle of less than 90° from the horizon. Or, we may say that the sun's meridian altitude reaches a maximum of 90° and stands at the zenith at noon every day somewhere within the latitudes of the tropics, between approx. 23° 28′N. lat. and 23° 28′S. lat. In the northern mid-summer (June 21–23) the earth is turned so that the sun is directly over the Tropic of Cancer, and the north polar regions are then also turned continuously towards the sun. Six months later (December 21–23) the sun shines directly down on the latitude of the Tropic of Capricorn, and the south polar regions are enjoying twenty-four hours of daylight. A careful examination of the diagrams makes these seasonal changes quite clear; they occur because the earth, moving round the sun in its annual course, maintains a constant inclination to the plane of its orbit. Again, for most readers, my diagram may be more explicit than my words.

Moreover, the fact that the noon sun is always low in the polar regions (and lower still at other times of day!)—so low in mid-winter that it doesn't even lift above the horizon—means that its rays must strike these regions obliquely and, consequently, by longer paths through the earth's atmosphere than at lower (nearer the equator) latitudes. A simple analogy may help. If a nail were passed vertically through a horizontal board it would encounter less total resistance than if it were driven at an angle. Or, lay a ruler (representing the sun's parallel rays) across two parallel lines, or arcs, representing the atmosphere and the surface of the earth. If the direction of the ruler is kept constant as it is moved across the arcs and, at intervals, rays are drawn, it will be clearly seen how they vary in the angle they make with the surface arc, and in the distance they travel through 'the atmosphere'. The obliquity of the sun's rays is the fundamental reason for the low temperatures at and near the poles.

However, the Antarctic is a great deal colder than the Arctic, so, obviously, there must be another factor or factors. Altitude is the next consideration. The greater part of the Arctic carries sea-level atmospheric pressures; Antarctica rises to heights at which re-radiation of solar energy, whether received directly, or by wind or ocean currents, is facilitated by the clear rarified air of the high plateau. That the surface of Antarctica comprises the world's broadest, brightest reflector, its gleaming white surface radiating heat into space, is a concomitant factor. Once a surface is deeply ice-covered the consequent reflection from the white surface helps keep the temperature low. In this respect an ice-cap is self sustaining. A third, also complex, reason for Antarctica's frigidity is its great interior distances from the moderating effects of the sea. Except for the narrow coastal fringe, there is no part of the antarctic continent where the air temperature ever rises above 0°C. The mean annual temperatures are the lowest on earth. On several occasions inland winter temperatures falling to −75°C have been recorded. By comparison, the Arctic is mild; in summer it may be hot, humid and mosquito-ridden. Although the inland winter temperatures of Siberia and northern Canada may fall very low, the summer heat in the same places may allow prolific plant and animal life.

In the northern hemisphere several systems have been devised for defining the Arctic, the polar characteristics of which extend far, but irregularly, into the

Mask of ice. The blizzard mask being worn by this expeditioner has become totally covered with ice except at apertures for seeing and breathing.

Lenticular cloud, Heard Island. This great eddy cloud, formed in the lee of mountainous Heard Island, retains its form although powerful winds are constantly transporting its substance. [A.C.-D.]

A bare rock wall in the David Range. Many antarctic mountains show faces bare of snow because they are too cold and dry for blizzards to deposit it.

Scene in the Masson Range, Framnes Mountains, MacRobertson Land.

The summits of mountains buried by the plateau drift. Many such ranges occur in most parts of Antarctica, near the coast especially. Further inland whole ranges may be completely covered.

northern continents. Areas of permanently frozen soil ('permafrost') and of treeless tundras are often cited as truly arctic. But the treeline may vary between the 55th and 70th north parallels of latitude, while areas of permafrost are extraordinarily sporadic, in parts of Canada and Siberia occurring south of the 50th parallel. The definition of the Antarctic is less difficult. It is circumpolar and oceanic, limited by the movement of drifting pack ice and, especially, by the zone known as the Antarctic Convergence, where the cold, less saline and denser surface waters surrounding the continent sink below the warmer waters of greater salinity and of tropical and sub-tropical origins. The convergence is irregular and variable, but lies in latitudes between 50°S. (round most of Eastern Antarctica) and below 60°S. (dipping in several places in the Pacific sector). Of particular significance is the fact that the Antarctic Convergence is an approximate boundary for much planktonic life. It includes the sub-antarctic islands; the Ballenys, Macquarie, Heard, the Kerguelens, Bouvet, South Sandwich, South Georgia and others. Although the temperature change at the convergence is slight—from 8°C–10°C in the south-flowing water to 4°C–6°C for that from higher latitudes, the effect is often noticeable. The crossing of the convergence has sometimes coincided in calm clear weather with a slight appearance of 'frost-smoke' vapour resulting from the cooling of warmer saturated air—and, before long, of floating ice.

In the milder coastal climate the scientific stations of Eastern Antarctica, those on, or a little south of, the Antarctic Circle, such as Molodezhnaya (USSR), Mawson and Davis (Australia), or Dumont D'Urville (France), enjoy *mean annual* temperatures of under −12°C. Minimum temperatures may drop to −40°C but, along this coast in an afternoon of high summer it may rise to +1°C or even +2°C for an hour or so. One Mawson team boasted that their station was situated in the 'Riviera' of the Antarctic. However, only a hundred or so kilometres inland the mean annual temperature everywhere drops sharply to −20°C; then, by roughly parallel isotherms in steps of 10°C, until the main central plateau, lying entirely in Eastern Antarctica and including the South Pole, an area of about 2 000 000 square kilometres, experiences an average of −50°C. The 80th south parallel precisely divides this area of intense cold. For the sake of comparison with the northern polar regions, Spitzbergen, in lat. 80°N. has an annual mean temperature of −8°C, that is 42°C warmer.

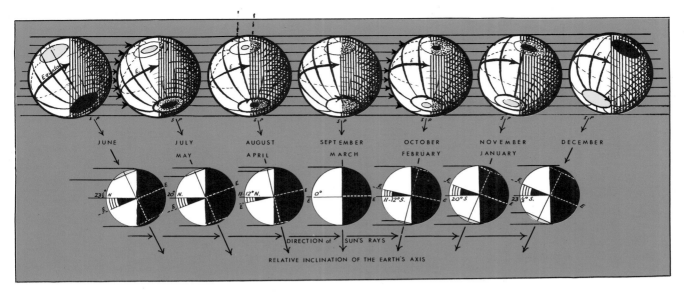

JUNE   JULY   AUGUST   SEPTEMBER   OCTOBER   NOVEMBER   DECEMBER

MAY   APRIL   MARCH   FEBRUARY   JANUARY

DIRECTION of SUN'S RAYS

RELATIVE INCLINATION OF THE EARTH'S AXIS

The lower figure demonstrates the unchanging inclination of the earth's axis to the plane of its orbit, and its constant variation relative to the direction of the sun. This variation causes the sun's change of inclination (its 'declination') north or south of the plane of the equator, as shown in the upper diagrams. Between the two extremes of 23½°N. and 23½°S. declination, the polar circles oscillate between periods of midwinter noon darkness and midsummer midnight sun. The larger ovals show the Arctic and Antarctic Circles; the smaller concentric ovals represent the areas of continuous night and day varying with the seasons. The lengths of day and night in each season, at various latitudes, are shown by the proportion of light and shade on any parallel. The seven smaller circles correspond to the globes sketched above, and show diagrammatically the sun's varying declination and the consequent changes in the 'circles of illumination' at the poles. The globes are represented as they would be seen from orbital positions ahead of (and slightly 'below') the earth, which is thus shown with its sunlit hemisphere regularly on the left.

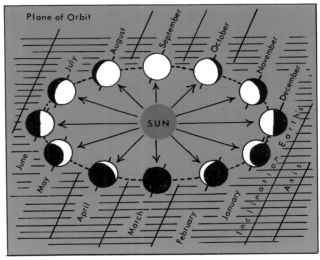

Outliers of the Prince Charles Mountains, MacRobertson Land.

I can recall a quiet walk round the South Pole, trying to keep a uniform distance from a circle of drums which the Americans had set up to mark 90° South as accurately as they could. The sun shone brilliantly all day, with no apparent change in its altitude as it moved imperceptibly round the horizon. There was no breath of wind, but I had clothed myself fully with windproof parka and balaclava and, tucked under it, a blizzard mask as a kind of insurance. I wore my gloves in their harness. The temperature was −52°C. I experimented by spitting and my saliva was ice as it hit the surface.

It is not difficult to discover the mean annual temperature anywhere on the plateau. Summer and winter temperatures vary most near the surface, but with depth the variation becomes less, since the lower *névé* is shielded to an increasing extent from both seasonal extremes. At about twelve metres the *névé* holds the approximate mean between the two. As an example, 160 kilometres south of the coast near Mawson, a reading at depth gave −29°C, approximately the same as the mean annual temperature on the surface at this point. The minimum on the surface here might be between twenty and twenty-five degrees lower. Scott's lowest temperature on his polar journey was −43.3°C, on 10 March 1912, on the Ross Ice Shelf, not long before his death.

Cold is only one element of weather. By itself, even at temperatures well below zero, it does not constitute a factor of any great discomfort to human beings properly dressed and healthy, for the warm layer of air generated near the skin is not disturbed without wind. If the sun is shining and the air is calm, the flesh absorbs and re-radiates heat of a kind that warms the air in immediate contact with the skin. If this is not disturbed, one may feel pleasantly warm and even tempted to sunbathe at temperatures several degrees

below freezing point. Once or twice each summer, certainly at the 'Riviera' stations, such conditions usually occur briefly, and it is a memorable sight and sensation —men reclining in the benign reflected glare of a metal-sheathed wall, with immense snowdrifts hard and dry beside them, and the rocks too cold still to sustain an animated trickle. Though the trickles may also appear in a still noon. An amusing memory is of ten-month husky pups, thereto snowfed, meeting their first liquid water, tentatively advancing paws to touch the strange shining fluid and prancing back in alarm. At the South Pole one day in October I saw the venue of a voluntary

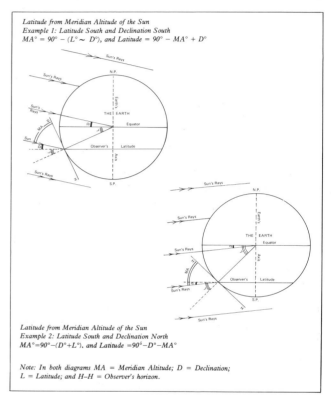

Latitude from Meridian Altitude of the Sun
Example 1: Latitude South and Declination South
$MA° = 90° − (L° \sim D°)$, and Latitude $= 90° − MA° + D°$

Latitude from Meridian Altitude of the Sun
Example 2: Latitude South and Declination North
$MA° = 90° − (D° + L°)$, and Latitude $= 90° − D° − MA°$

Note: In both diagrams MA = Meridian Altitude; D = Declination; L = Latitude; and H–H = Observer's horizon.

Mawson station photographed from the western arm of the harbour. [M.C.]

and unofficial experiment to see how one fared in a swift transition from −50°C to +50°C. With a steaming tub ready at the latter temperature one of the company made a momentary dry dash into the still and arid air and returned swiftly to the warmth of the bath. Without harm and naked he had run a gamut of degrees of temperature equal to that between the freezing and boiling points of fresh water. Terrestrial temperatures may range much further, but such experiments are not recommended.

It is inanimate substances that best indicate low temperatures in still air. At −35°C, a candle may leave a little cylinder of lacy wax round half the flame; butter splinters like a stone; tepid water thrown out of doors freezes as it touches the rock or ice and forms heaps; fish drawn through a hole in the ice give a convulsive

Seal at breathing hole in thick sea-ice. The Weddell seal survives below the winter ice by keeping open a breathing hole. Several breathing holes may exist in a few square kilometres.

Drift snow streaming through the station at Mawson. [G.H.]

shiver, freeze solid and are quite brittle in a few minutes after reaching the air. The water below the ice, of course, must be at a temperature above freezing; so it is maintained for the comfort of the midwinter marine residents by the insulation of the floating ice. Were ice to sink, instead of floating as it does, the world might be a frozen, uninhabitable planet.

Husky dogs are rare today, having given way to machines, and those that remain are mostly fed on imported food, but once, large numbers of seals were shot for dog food. The stock-piled carcasses, frozen hard, were sawn with a cross-cut into huge cutlets of dog food, and the husky pups came over, if they were allowed, to lick up the sawdust. The cutlets were split with an axe, precisely like sections of a tree trunk. Metals cause painful frost-burns if they are handled at these temperatures. Mercury freezes into a solid, malleable metal at approx. −40°C. At the same temperature tin tends to disintegrate[49] and many metals become very brittle. For most of the year all water required at stations for domestic purposes is either quarried from a convenient drift or glacier face and melted down indoors, or carted from a distance in solid or liquid form. Sometimes there are convenient seasonal meltwater pools against rock faces which have absorbed considerable solar radiation; in many cases electric immersion heaters are used to melt their own reservoirs of liquid water which is then pumped or otherwise transported to the station.

Nothing, I think, so impresses the Antarctican with a sense of isolation and solitude as the freezing sea. A curious lack-lustre glaze first seems to damp all sparkle; this thin film may thicken to mushy 'brash', graduate to a special beauty as 'pancake', often most reminiscent of those immense water-lily leaves of the Victoria *regia* species (strange jungle nadir of the scene!), and then, inevitably, coalesce, thicken more and still the most tempestuous seas for anything up to ten months of the

year. But for the tidal hinging and pressure ridging at the shoreline, one might believe the sea were dead. The retention of interstitial brine adds plasticity to young ice but, as this salt content lessens, especially late in the season, the faintly wimpled surface may become polished by dry wind-blown snow. Occasionally, I have skated unbounded on a lonely sea-rink, using long steel skates forged and ground from a leaf of a tractor spring. Usually there was impedance from residual salt crystals which, in less severe frost, would mostly have been drained away as brine through the ice crystals.[50] There is no more heartening phenomenon in nature than the yearly break-up of the fast ice into floes and their drifting away as pack to the northern horizon.

Unless a person has lived through the seasons within the astronomical limits of a polar Circle and experienced not only the midnight sun and the midday darkness but the slow transition of one to the other, his appreciation of some aspects is likely to be academic. As the axis of the hemisphere changes its angle to the sun's parallel rays[51] from a maximum of 113½°, when all areas within the Circle are in darkness (being screened by the curvature of the earth), to its opposite extreme of inclination (66½°) when all areas within the Circle are sunlit, any day is likely to provide a quality of skylight and colour unmatched in lower latitudes. Tropical sunsets and dawns are always swift and sometimes violent of colour; in polar regions they may endure for hours in a strange tranquillity, so that it seems almost as though time itself were arrested. Often, while an apricot flush of distant day still lingers on the horizon, the aurora will pulsate over the darkening sky; the effect is one of quite unearthly beauty.

Between the equinoxes (approximately from 21 September to 21 March) the sun never sets at the South Pole; it remains just swinging round the sky, first in circles of increasing altitude until the maximum (23½°)[52] is reached on midsummer day; then in decreasing altitudes—imperceptible to the eye from day to day—until it again slides round the horizon in March and slowly continues as a daylong sunset, finally dropping below the horizon until only the faintest midwinter flush is left in June to encircle the dark disc of the visible world. The strictly polar phenomena are unique, but the seasons of the two hemispheres of course differ in time by six months.

The freezing sea; this 'oily' appearance is an early sign of low temperatures at sea, and the 'damping effect' of ice is apparent even at this stage.

Nuclei enlarge as the freezing of the sea continues, the slower the freezing the less salt entrapped in the interstices of the ice.

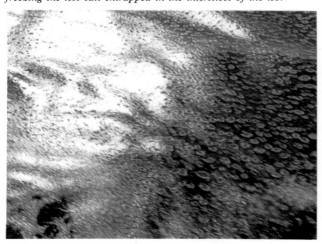

Typical 'pancake' ice. Later these 'pancakes' will coalesce and form continuous ice which may, however, be broken up several times before it thickens sufficiently to last through the winter.

Icicles draping the side of a melt-water pool in coastal ice.

A fall of ice from the cliffs at the coast of Antarctica, scattered over the sea-ice. The land-ice long under pressure seems to spread with almost explosive violence.

Tide cracks opening in the coastal ice are an early sign of annual ice break-up.

Casey station, Wilkes Land, Antarctica. This construction, to minimize the accumulation of drift snow, has suffered from vibration. All antarctic stations continue to be experimental, they range from geodesic domes, through under-ice living quarters and laboratories, to relatively drift-free constructions raised on stilts. [G.F.]

Nearer the antarctic coast, with latitude decreasing, the period of continuous midsummer sunlight becomes less and less until, a little northwards of the Antarctic Circle, there is no day when the sun actually shines through midnight.[53] However, anywhere near or within the Circle the summer days are long and the twilight either before or after the sun's actual appearance is wonderfully protracted. All night the flush of the sun is visible somewhere in the sky, burnishing icebergs far out at sea or resting gloriously on some distant peak or glacier along the coast. It is easy to calculate the midday altitude of the sun (its elevation in degrees above the horizon) for any locality on any day by computing a resultant angle[54] from the latitude and the sun's declination.

The protracted sunlight of the polar summer does more than merely balance the effects of the winter darkness. The sun's altitude and prolonged presence allow warming of ice, air and sea and the occurrence of stable conditions and consequent effects over seasonal periods. Dark rock, where it is exposed, absorbs radiant solar heat and, in turn, warms the air by re-radiation.[55] The intense winter cold, permitting the sea to freeze, is offset by the continuous heating which disintegrates the sea-ice in summer. However, in the opinion of a noted authority on the subject[56] it is only for about two months in midsummer (November and December) that the south polar snow collects more energy from the sun than it radiates into space. The annual deficit, he claims, is made good by atmospheric heat from solar energy, conveyed by air movements from lower latitudes. By such means is the earth's energy budget kept in balance. The tilt of the earth, of course, is responsible for seasonal changes in all latitudes. Without this tilt and the consequent seasons it is probable that the polar ice-caps, if they existed, would be much restricted; life on the Equator, on the other hand, might be unendurable. Days would always be of the same length all over the world, and there would be little local variation in weather from one year's end to another; latitude and the configuration of landmasses and oceans would be the main determinants of change.

It might be inferred that the solar relations of our planet, in general constant from year to year, should do no more than balance their seasonal effects. This is not strictly so, since an accumulation of winter snow, with strong albedo, will tend to retain its temperature and reflect incident solar radiation. Thus there is an argument for the persistence of snowfields once, for any reason, a season of unusual precipitation occurs; likewise a period of unusual thaw may so thin a field of *névé* that subsequent summers expose more and more rock. For some time, all over the world, it seems that glaciers and perhaps the Greenland ice-cap have been receding. Long-term cycles have, according to geological evidence, occurred in the past, and this recession may be part of such a one. Though the effects may be evaluated, the causes remain unknown. We cannot explain all apparent anomalies. Fortunately we cannot conceive mankind as having no challenge to face, no field to explore, no gap to fill in his slow, eternal search for understanding of his environment, let alone himself.

It should be appreciated that the snow of intensely cold conditions is finer, lighter and drier than that of relatively warmer climates; it will therefore not stay where it falls but will (in the case of the Antarctic) be blown northward, perhaps hundreds of kilometres, out to sea. Likewise, temperature will affect the plasticity of many substances, including ice, so that a lowering of temperature may cause a diminution of glacial flow.

The actual snowfall in Antarctica is remarkably small. It is also difficult to estimate owing to the effects of wind which, even in a dense blizzard, will often erode a surface, diminishing rather than raising a snow level. This effect is frequently demonstrated by the characteristic way in which tracks of men, dogs and sledges are left in high relief where the looser surrounding snow has been blown away. Millions of tonnes of snow are annually shifted from great distances over areas where the annual deposition is only a few centimetres. Of Adélie Land, it was estimated[57] that on each day of heavy blizzard an average of 380 000 tonnes of snow passed out over the sea for each 1.6 kilometre of coastline. On the Ross Ice Shelf one estimate of total average precipitation has been reckoned to be equivalent to twenty centimetres of rain—a desert rainfall. However, the estimates from many observations and measurements and what seems logical extrapolation

reveal much lower precipitation over most of the continent. Stakes set up as snow gauges, interpreted with estimates of the quantities of snow lost by all forms of ablation, provide one set of measurements. Another set of absolute readings comes from measurements of annual striae revealed in the walls of carefully excavated pits, and in core samples from drilling, all again to be modified by estimated ablation. It is obviously easier to measure accumulation than ablation, and there has never been a consensus of opinion amongst glaciologists concerning the mass economy—whether the ice of the Antarctic is, in the long term, increasing or decreasing. There is some reason to suppose that the accumulation and loss are in balance, the one therefore being deducible from the other. The volume of the total land-based ice in Antarctica has been reckoned at 24 000 000 cubic kilometres, the annual ice supplement at 2 400 cubic kilometres, and the mass loss in the form of icebergs at half this accumulation.[58] Today it is possible by satellite imagery to monitor the size and number of icebergs breaking away from the coast and the edges of ice shelves. It is generally agreed that they constitute by far the greatest loss. Ocean levels have been slowly rising at the rate of 1.2 millimetres per year.[59] Does the Antarctic contribute to this rise?

In cold climates snowfall is directly proportional to temperature; that is, less snow falls as it becomes colder. Antarctic air is extremely dry, its absolute moisture content being low whatever its percentage of relative humidity (i.e. the water vapour it can sustain at any particular temperature). So the precipitation map of Antarctica, the snowfall being shown as equivalent

Macquarie Island station in winter dusk. [R.T.]

centimetres of rain, shows a close relation with the map of isotherms, the huge area of the five centimetre isohyet—the largest area of such low precipitation in the world—easily contains the area of lowest temperature.

Wind is by far the most potent element in Antarctica. It converts loose snow into a howling, spiteful blizzard; the bewildering and dangerous white darkness that immobilizes, to a degree, all travellers and all means of transport. So drastically does it increase the effects of cold on human beings, by removing the superficial warm air trapped by the pores and hairs of the skin, by surface evaporation, and by disturbance of cushioned air held by clothing, that every knot of wind has been considered by some as being equal, in terms of human discomfort, to a fall of one degree in temperature. It is certain that −20°C, in calm conditions with the sun shining can be pleasant, but that much higher

Digging out the tent after the night's blizzard.

Light blizzard drift, antarctic plateau.

Taut drifts form in the lee of huts. They are often separated from the walls by wind-scours.

Glacier camp, Heard Island.

temperatures, even above zero, may be difficult to endure in a gale of wind, the chances of actual frostbite being infinitely higher.[60]

Frostbite is insidious; it occurs without warning and without pain. On the face superficial frostbite is frequent when factors of temperature and wind react to cause freezing of exposed flesh. It shows itself as paper-white patches on cheeks, nose and ears (if they are exposed), but is easily dissipated by a little massage from a gloved hand cupping a warm breath. However, the subject does not feel the frostbite and usually in a party, one warns his fellows of its occurrence. Serious frostbite of the extremities may happen without the subject being aware of his danger. A frozen heel may give the impression that one is walking on the ball of the foot, but all sensation may depart from frozen toes or fingers. I once had an index finger frozen to an ice-axe, without being aware of the torn glove or the insensible fingertip. Serious frostbite must receive external warmth, preferably from immersion in warm water, though the pain of thawing may be intense. In the field

men have often provided warmth for a frostbitten sufferer with their bodies. Rubbing a frostbitten area with snow, as once advised, will intensify the injury.

Wind pressure rises very steeply with velocity.[61] While a gale of 80 kilometres per hour[62] will exert a pressure of approximately 37 kilograms per square metre, a hurricane of 160 kilometres per hour will exert four times that force. Provided one has sufficient foot

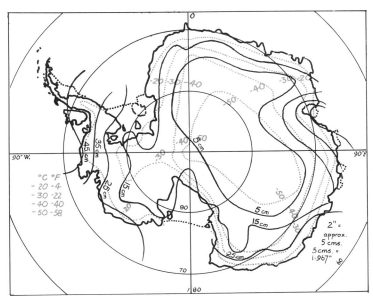

Mean annual temperatures and mean annual accumulation in Antarctica. The black curves connect regions of approximately the same mean annual snow accumulation, i.e. total precipitation less ablation by wind, evaporation etc. The black figures express the equivalents in inches of water. It will be realized that, in these terms, Antarctica receives precipitation equivalent to that of a desert. Over much of Antarctica the total ablation would account for a mean loss of about one inch. The coloured curves represent isotherms showing approximate mean annual temperatures in degrees Celsius. Conversion tables are shown for, respectively, inches to centimetres, and degrees Celsius to degrees Fahrenheit.

Hoar frost on vehicle window. [M.P.]

Cosmic-ray telescope at Mawson station.

The snow run. When all other systems fail, a station's fresh-water supply must be quarried and carried to the snow-melters. Many hands make light work. [M.C.]

Ice-cores on sledge, inland from Casey station. [K.G.]

Patterns of drift, near Davis station.

anchorage (on ice by means of sharp crampons—steel spikes strapped to the boots), it is possible to learn to struggle against such blasts, leaning at an angle which appears gravitationally absurd. The really high gusts may be extremely destructive, their pressures ranging upwards to more than 500 kilograms per square metre. This, of course, is why antarctic huts must be so strong and so well guyed: the wall of a small building, twelve square metres in area, might receive a sudden total pressure of something over five tonnes. In one of the most destructive antarctic hurricanes I ever experienced we lost two *Beaver* aircraft, dismembered of wings and tail-planes and torn to pieces, although they were firmly anchored to the plateau ice, turned into the wind and equipped with 'wind-spoilers' to interrupt the air-flow. When after a desperate struggle, we had made them as secure as was humanly possible, we crawled cramponed into a massive sledge-caravan with runners frozen deep into the ice which served as the airfield's operational headquarters. The storm increased until its gusts exceeded 300 kilometres per hour. Even our firmly held refuge seemed insecure, but there was no possibility of our leaving it. So we watched helplessly through a small double-glazed plate window, as a main plane even was detached from an aircraft and carried away bodily, like a blown leaf. We had mapped many thousands of kilometres with those planes.

With wind usually rises drift, and with drift, humidity and frequently temperature because of its absorption of solar radiation and reflected heat from the surface. In the combination of these factors, through the temperature range of antarctic blizzards, lies danger and discomfort unless adequate shelter is available. It is certain that blizzard was a contributing factor, with deficiencies of diet and unsuitable transport, to the tragic end of Scott's expedition. If a party is immobilized—by the weather itself, or because it is impossible to navigate, or by dangerous crevassing in the area—then its food and fuel resources are taxed. In the case of Scott's party, very low temperatures (averaging −40°C for weeks), inadequate food and hard manhauling were the prime causes of disaster; their last hopes of reaching a depot, only a day's march away, were removed by blizzard. I have already mentioned the odd psychological effect blizzard has for some, of causing intense introspection, as though the white sea through which one stumbles dimensionless, deprived of sight and, by insulation, of sensation, exerted hypnotic influence.

Strong winds are more common in Antarctica, especially round the coast, than anywhere else on earth. The velocities of winds blowing down from the plateau may reach 125 kilometres to 160 kilometres an hour, and may continue uniformly high for considerable periods; brief gusts may rise to 240 kilometres or more per hour. Such hurricanes may occur anywhere round the coast, and frequently they appear to cross the low-lying trough of Antarctica between the Ross and Weddell Seas. In Eastern Antarctica, with distance inland, the winds decrease in violence. Records from the various national stations prove that some experience more constant wind than others, and that, in the interior calms are more common than near the sea. Mawson's second winter season, in 1913, at his Cape Denison base, just east of Adélie Land, was one of the stormiest ever recorded. On 5 July, the wind all day held an average of 171 kilometres per hour. The entire month's average was 101.38 kilometres and, for the year, about

80 kilometres per hour. A famous photograph, reproduced on the original cover of *The Home of the Blizzard*,[63] and with the text, shows Eric Webb, the expedition's geomagnetician, leaning on the wind at what seems an impossible angle. The Adélie Land area has consistently maintained its reputation. By contrast, at the Australian station named after Mawson, in long. 62° 53′E., an average wind-speed of only half that recorded at Cape Denison was registered in a typical June. At Mawson, the average period of severe storms is shorter than at Mirni, the USSR base only eight hundred kilometres from Davis, and about the same again from Mawson. Stations round the coast 'hand on' weather in a clockwise, easterly direction, but each area seems to contribute its special qualitites. A storm at Syowa, the Japanese station for instance, will reach Mawson in two or three days, and thence be on its way to Davis, Mirni and Casey (see map).

In general terms the pattern of weather in Antarctica is part of an atmospheric cycle extending between the Equator and the South Pole, in which north-bound air, dense, cold and at low levels, deflected to the west by the rotation of the earth,[64] streams out from Antarctica to compensate for large masses of less dense, warmer tropical air, moving south at great heights and partly deflected eastward by the West Wind Drift. Below is the Antarctic Convergence; the Drift, as a similar movement in the northern hemisphere, is associated with jet streams of high altitude and speeds. Naturally the fluidity of air and water make them the transporters of heat energy; although what we usually call 'the weather' concerns the lowest few kilometres of the atmosphere, the grand strategy of compensation extends to the immensely powerful currents at heights of many kilometres. All wind is caused primarily by temperature differences in air resulting in irregularities of atmospheric pressure. The tropics hold dark, heat-absorbing surfaces—earth, vegetation, rock, sea—re-radiating this heat to raise the temperature of highly humidified air, while the polar regions, relatively, are small, radiating heat energy into space, lowering the temperature on the high plateau in places to −85°C.[65] So the imbalance is obvious; the tropical heat belt occupies twelve times the area of each of the polar regions within their respective circles of midnight sun. Somehow the blending and the balance must be achieved; this entails a colossal flow of energy towards the poles. However, as we have seen, the imbalance is immeasurably greater in the southern hemisphere.[66] Immense storms of moist air, shedding rain or snow

Most of Byrd, an IGY station constructed by the USA at the intersection of the 120th west meridian and the 80th south parallel, was subnévéan. The observatories had tabular access to the under-ice station.

At the South Pole Amundsen-Scott station. A large geodesic dome covers several of the buildings.

Auroral curtains. [D.P.]

Night Sky. [T.]

as they are caught by the movement of the earth and swirled eastward, race into Antarctica; the compensating airflow, lifting the dry snow in blizzard clouds, pours down the slopes of the great white dome. And, with all the complexities of detail, the thermal balance of the earth is maintained; the sun's energy, having fulfilled its vast functions, is sent back into space. If, as the Eskimoes have it, 'Weather and Ice are kings!' the sun is emperor!

Scientists and observers, living in their silver villages round the antarctic coasts, are naturally apt to think of weather as epitomized by the furious gravitational ('katabatic') winds on which they lean as they grope their way along the rope blizzard lines through the white darkness. Torrential katabatic streams, however, are seldom deep, nor do they flow far out to sea. They may, naturally, augment greater geostrophic[67] systems. Where there are great estuaries or ice shelves, or where mountain ranges, below or above the ice, funnel the wind, there may be a concentration of its energy in what I have called 'weather streams', but all over Antarctica there are differences not easily linked with irregularities of surface or coastal configuration. My most memorable experiences of weather streams were provided by the powerful flow of opaque blizzardly air that often raced seaward above the Lambert Glacier and the Amery Ice Shelf. We frequently flew from bright clear sunshine into total opacity, and emerged into sunshine again on the far side of the aerial Amazon, or Amery Weather Stream.

It is tempting to leave the subject of weather while we are in the area of certainties but, continually, ever since the meteorologist with Scott's last expedition, Dr G. C. Simpson, proposed that a radial pressure wave system developed over Antarctica and accounted for disturbances over great distances, even beyond the Equator, there have been research and speculation on the major patterns of polar meteorology. Although there are still numerous different theories and opinions of detail, the many years of synoptic observations have buttressed his general theory, while the extraordinary breakthrough that has enabled satellite imagery of the immense twisting cyclones that ventilate Antarctica to be obtained daily, still further supports the hypothesis of total inter-relation of the weather systems of the hemisphere, if not of the world.

There is always a marked difference between the heating effects of the sea and of the ice, at the coast or at the varying edge of the pack ice, where there is a tendency for the warm air to rise over the cold. The interface is one frontal area which may move north or south, according to season and the balance of other systems, and profoundly affect the weather of more temperate latitudes. As we have seen there is yet another interface at the latitude of the Antarctic Convergence. At each front of this kind the warmer air probably rises and joins the southern movement, passing above such vigorous flows as the katabatics. There are boundaries between the two or more layers, maintained by their contrary movement as well as their differing densities. Not only the velocity, but the deflection of winds is variable; the former is affected by gravity and the magnitudes of pressure systems, and the latter by the changing rotational speed of the earth's surface, according to latitude. The cores of the deflection movement and of the temperature differential are not coincident; deflection is centred by the geographical pole, disappearing there entirely—at Eliot's 'still point of the turning earth'—while the 'cold pole' very high and remote from the sea, is close to the summit of the eastern lobe, near the USSR station of Vostok, where have been measured the lowest terrestrial temperatures. In this high area, of course, the incoming air has completed its cycle.

The winds leaving Antarctica, deflected west, are contained when they encounter the effect of the eastward drifting cyclones of relatively low pressure, constituting the important polar front we have already noticed. The westerly drift is held along the continental coast. My map, compiled from quite typical weather systems recorded by satellite technology,[68] explains more clearly than words the area of the polar front, its systems of processional cyclones surrounding the increasing stability of the daylight season. In summer a stable high-pressure anticyclone may persist over Eastern Antarctica.

Disturbances of a wave nature occur at the boundary or interface between two moving fluids of different densities. Such is typified, of course, by the waves caused by the wind over the surface of the sea. Once the movement commences it may increase its amplitude. According to the proposed pattern of antarctic air movements, there are two distinct boundaries where wave motion may be engendered: firstly that which separates the cold and warm layers of air over the continent[69] and, secondly, that existing at the polar front. At the former, radial waves like ripples on a round pond will be propagated; these will be seasonal, and vary with the pressures systems. Their main effect is to cause an oscillation—a seasonal shift—in the latitude of the polar storm barrier which may be communicated to the paths of 'highs and lows' in more temperate latitudes.

Meteorological chart: This chart shows how closely related are the weather systems of the Southern Hemisphere. Each set of concentric isobars shows either a low or high pressure area. The low pressure areas round Antarctica are cyclones swirling in a clockwise direction. They also move round the world from west to east, as does the West Wind Drift seen, with the Antarctic Convergence, clearly in this map. Satellites now greatly help meteorologists in observing such vast systems as this (which was plotted 11 October 1965 at McMurdo Sound).

The author's igloo on the high plateau, constructed to facilitate the micro-photography of snow crystals.

The movement at the perimeter of the system will generate 'scallop' waves in the polar front. The whole system may perhaps be pictured as a mass of cold air overlain and enclosed by a warm layer. The height of the major 'inversion' between the cold and warm air may range from two to four kilometres at the coast and progressively less inland. To complicate the picture there may be lesser inversions, some virtually at the surface of the ice, or only a few metres above. At the coast, the differences in the velocity and temperature of the air streams are found to be most marked, measurements being daily obtained by the use of radiosonde balloons carrying instruments that automatically transmit information on temperature, pressure and humidity to meteorologists on the ground, and from balloons tracked by radiotheodolite.

In the northern hemisphere the theory has been advanced, by Kochin and others, that scallop waves round the edge of the polar system periodically become unstable and break up into detached cyclonic disturbances, reaching southward and pouring arctic air into the more inhabited latitudes. Recent theories[70] associ-

Radiosonde release. The large hydrogen-filled balloon will carry meteorological instruments to great heights from which there is continuous transmission of data. [H.G.]

Meltwater pool. The falling water has left part of its former frozen surface. [W.J.R.D.]

ate such scallop waves in the north with eastward flowing jet-streams, and it is suggested that major changes in the pattern and magnitude of these movements may be responsible for long term climatic cycles. Changes in the atmospheric 'sun shield' are held greatly to influence long term change and, further back in the chain of causal sequence, sun spots and solar flares are again being investigated. We may observe and investigate the weather of the oceans and atmosphere and, by logical induction create our theories, or we may attempt bold leaping to conclusions. Dr Simpson's original hypothesis and all the amendments and corollaries of the century still have the same object, to explain the procession of short duration cyclonic disturbances continually moving eastward in the 'middle' latitudes of the southern oceans, the storm barrier that tosses all ships bound for Antarctica, and its effects on the rest of the southern hemisphere.

It is possible that, in some apparent anomalies, clues will be found to climatic cycles of much longer duration. Research will be continued not only into what happens, but at least some of the distance back along the eternal regress of why it should be so. Studies of antarctic weather will continue their unique contribution to our knowledge of the planet Earth.

Antarctica's influence on weather is, then, of world concern. In these days of national expeditions, of the Antarctic Treaty and regular meetings of the consultative parties to decide on policies of co-ordinating research and other matters of common interest, the antarctic explorer is a civil servant. He works within a world where science is essentially indivisible. Decades ago, in the IGY, there was established a living graticule of observers from pole to pole; it was set up in order that no political barriers should interrupt research; all results, it was declared, should be freely shared. In Antarctica, this co-operation still exists; all major research programmes are nationally funded. Traditional methods of gathering weather information have been augmented by all sorts of sophisticated aids; they measure the elements of weather—temperature, air-pressure and humidity—and they record its symptoms— wind, precipitation and cloud-cover. Carefully screened instruments at ground level; radio impulses from free-floating balloons rising to thirty thousand or more metres; satellites at altitudes of hundreds of

Tension crevassing, formed before they were calved, shows up clearly in this aerial view of two icebergs. They leave a clear wake as they drift through new ice.

Young sea-ice disturbed by a fall of plateau ice from the edge of an ice shelf.

kilometres; all contribute. Synopses of atmospheric data are co-ordinated, and produce clear pictures of systems, weather fronts and movements, all reconciled with satellite information. No less than their electronic informants, meteorologists in the field make essential contributions. They must follow rope lines through the white gloom of blizzard to reach their instruments; in sub-zero cold they must follow, through theodolite telescopes, the flight of small balloons indicating air movements. The hydrogen gas for these and the larger radiosonde[71] balloons is usually imported in cylinders landed with other supplies but, occasionally, it may still have to be generated on the station; heavy work requiring patience and acute watchfulness. To convert ice to the near boiling water required for the reaction may in itself be a major task. And then, in a gale of wind, to release the vulnerable balloons, one to two metres in diameter, with radiosonde transmitters attached, requires consummate technique. A false move in this game and much work and expensive equipment may be lost. Often for hours, the signals from the high distant balloon are received and recorded. The character of the effort required of antarctic scientists is difficult to convey to those who have not experienced life in high latitudes.

A number of meteorological out-stations usually function at varying distances from the bases. They record data automatically, but they must be visited and serviced periodically, and the sheets or tapes of recorder mechanisms must be renewed. Field work is often arduous, with journeys over the plateau or sea ice, or by aircraft. Incidentally, meteorological observations are made regularly on all field journeys of exploration.

Dog-sledging on sea-ice.

An island camp: pegging out the dogs.

Wholly automatic stations, propagating radio impulses which may be interpreted as weather information, are also widely established.

I have mentioned meteorology in some detail because weather is apparent to our senses and, obviously, it is the determinant of much of Antarctica's past and present nature. It is, however, not the only environmental component of the far south. Many branches of geophysics and of the earth sciences are pursued as national contributions to the world pool of knowledge.[72] Studies of the upper atmosphere, of radio physics and of cosmic radiation are studied in the natural laboratory of the Antarctic where magnetic fields are concentrated to provide particle paths for extraterrestrial energies. Affecting the earth and its inhabitants, all these factors, visible and invisible, are the media for our modern antarctic explorers.

For a very small part of man's existence as *homo sapiens*, he has been conscious of forces beyond those manifesting themselves to his senses. It is curious indeed that the decline of superstition and belief in gods, goblins and fairies has been contemporaneous with the growth of knowledge and faith, of and in energies invisible and impalpable. The old gods of sunshine, wind, rain and fertility in the fields have been replaced by modern meteorology and agricultural science. The modern conception of matter, paradoxically—mass being equated with energy—is one of non-material forces. The list of energies possessing no gross manifestation, and of which we have no perceptual sense, has lengthened far beyond the belief of mediaeval man, intrigued and bewildered by the lodestone (though, perhaps oddly, taking gravitational forces for granted). Antarctica provides some of our best opportunities to probe those invisible, inaudible and impalpable aspects of our environment.

Geomagnetism is a science that must be studied all over the earth, but there are important foci in the Arctic

Crevasses near Casey. The slumped bridges are being tested; they screen the depths often many metres below. More dangerous, of course, is crevassing completely hidden under new snow. [R.O'L.]

Crevassed ice discovered by a tractor. This vehicle was prevented from sinking further by the use of long wooden planks carried for the purpose. [H.J.E.]

and the Antarctic—the magnetic poles which, curiously it might seem, are by no means constant. Since the existence of these areas was conceived, where a magnetic needle tends to point vertically into the surface of the earth, and their positions were first calculated, they have moved many hundreds of kilometres. It will be recalled that the urgent ambition of James Clark

Aerial panorama in the Prince Charles Mountains at the head of the Lambert Glacier and the Amery Ice Shelf.

The Scullin Monolith, with the frozen sea in the foreground and the plateau ice. This distinctive coastal feature is in long. approximately 66°E.

Ross, in 1840–41, was to reach the South Magnetic Pole, so balancing his success in the Arctic. Actually, by the time the area was attained by David, Mawson and Mackay, in 1909, it had migrated by a circuitous route from Gauss's calculated position of 1839 (76°S., 146°E.), northward and east by four degrees of latitude and nine of longitude. Continuing its cyclic movement, by the 1890s it was virtually at the coast near Mawson's Commonwealth Bay—a movement of seven hundred kilometres in much less than a century. Annually, in terms of change in magnetic declination all over the world, the movement is slight and fairly constant over long periods, but is necessarily assessed for navigational purposes. The magnetic behaviour of the earth is such as one might envisage if a great bar magnet were inside the earth wobbling round the spin axis—itself not quite constant. The shift of the 'dip pole' appears a local and superficial phenomenon; in space the focus is more constant. So we may consider the earth as possessing two 'dip poles'—the North and South Magnetic Poles—and two so-called 'geomagnetic poles', the theoretical approximations of the earth's magnetic fields, at which are centred associated or related phenomena. Extending far into space, and capable of deflecting and capturing streams of particles from the sun or outer space, the earth's magnetic field is sufficiently comprehended to allow the formulation of plausible theories. The Van Allen radiation belts, in which charged particles from the 'solar wind' are entrapped and accelerated, appear to extend the earth's magnetic influence thousands of kilometres into space. Much closer to earth, the intense polar magnetic fields, between which solar particles

Volcanic boulders, sculpted by wind, shattered by frost and painted by lichens are common at sea-level on Heard Island.

Massive erratic boulder split by frost, Mawson.

oscillate and spiral along lines of force, allow some electrons and protons to escape. Colliding with atoms and molecules of the outer atmosphere, these release their energy as visible light and produce the aurora.

The vast cage of magnetic energy is thought to be almost entirely of terrestrial origin; a small percentage, associated with the electrified ionosphere—a layer of the upper stratosphere—may be induced. But, in the manner of the lines of force demonstrable by a simple bar magnet and iron filings, those of the earth converge to the poles and deflect thither cosmic and solar particles. Therefore high latitudes constitute important areas for scientific observation of broadly related phenomena. As in meteorology, the storms, the anomalies and the unusual surges, upsetting the normal course and patterns of events, provide the best opportunities for learning more of their nature and of this invisible environment.

Sensitive instruments have been devised to record fluctuations in terrestrial magnetism, both seasonal, perhaps caused by slippage between the mantle and the fluid core of the earth, and diurnal—daily—caused by changes in the ionosphere and, ultimately, in the sun and its 'solar wind' of charged particles ejected into space with the continually expanding corona.[73] Continuous observations all over the world, timed with the utmost precision, prove that magnetic 'storms' are frequently of simultaneous onset.

Mount Olsen and the Laurens Peninsula, Heard Island.

In the Antarctic, especially in a well-known belt approximately surrounding the geomagnetic pole and at a distance of some twenty-three degrees—about 2 500 kilometres—auroral displays of varying intensities are usually visible whenever there is darkness and clear weather. The auroral physicist, preoccupied as he must be by considerations of the spatial and temporal distribution of this particular manifestation of energy, is nevertheless conscious of the direct appeal to the imagination of the colours, forms and movements of the spectacle. Bows of pulsating pale green light span the horizon, break up into rays, re-gather and form curtains and ribbons with incredible speed, become tinged with crimson, occasionally with violet, move restlessly over the stars, sometimes even outshining them. Although the forms of the aurora may be classified, and the causes may be explicable, the sight of the sky streaming with light is always astonishing and, to the majority of people, awesome. As visible symptoms of ionospheric conditions, as correlatives of magnetic storm and radio disturbance, the aurorae, both *borealis* and *australis*, will continue to be investigated quite dispassionately, but, as natural phenomena of surpassing beauty and majesty, they will always be exciting to anyone who winters in high latitudes.

Often I have stood at one end of a base-line many kilometres long, from each end of which angles of elevation provided the necessary triangulation for discovering the height of salient features of the aurora. Mostly these could also be photographed by an 'all-sky' camera. Whenever I could I wandered out onto the harbour ice just to experience what then seemed an orchestration of light, subtle draperies attuned to the music of the spheres, an experience when every observer is alone.

The various electrified layers of the ionosphere, at heights of between a hundred and six hundred kilometres reflect radio waves of differing frequencies and enable short-wave signals to be reflected over great distances, in a series of bounces between them and the earth's surface. Solar activity, modifying or intensifying the arrival of electrons in the ionosphere, may affect this reflection of radio signals and cause, instead, their

Depot Peak, between Mawson and the Prince Charles Mountains.

absorption. Such radio 'blackouts' are most noticeable in high latitudes. Ionospheric changes are regularly monitored to enable the most efficient frequencies to be selected as necessary for world-wide communication systems. Radio blackouts in the Antarctic are often accompanied by unusually vivid aurorae and strong magnetic disturbances. It is obvious that all these phenomena must be studied in themselves, as well as for any technical benefits conferred on mankind. Yet there is inspiration in the thought that ionospheric research was the father of modern radar.

Another energy reaching the earth is that of 'cosmic rays', particles entering the earth's atmosphere at high velocities from outer space and undergoing nuclear change before reaching its surface. The study of cosmic radiation has added to man's knowledge of atomic, and especially of nuclear, physics, indeed to his conception and comprehension of physical substance. The advances of the last half-century, the frightening power of atomic weapons, the vision of man's control over resources undreamed of in the youth of our fathers, culminating in the release of energy from the fission or fusion of elements—all are related to contributions from the studies of cosmic radiation. The primary cosmic particles affect and are affected by the atoms of the earth's upper atmosphere. There transmutation may take place: in that far attenuated space is a seminary for the atomic physicist. It was the investigation of 'natural' radioactivity and its ensuing transmutations which led to the Joliots' discovery of 'artificial' radioactivity in 1934.

I have done little more than hint at the vast and complex scientific programme of the nations interested in Antarctica. The knowledge sought is not easier to obtain than that concerning the tangible nature and resources of the continent. Those expedition members whose task is geology, glaciology or mapping are explorers in visible media. They will eventually know how Antarctica is formed and what minerals exist there both above and below its ice, and along the deep continental shelf; they will continue investigating ice movement, thickness, and its general heat and mass economy; how precisely it is shaped in every direction. All these are being investigated with ever more sophisticated devices. The geologist has his geiger counters and scintillometers (which detect radioactive areas from the air), and he makes use of knowledge of anomalies in gravitational and geomagnetic forces to discover variations in crustal structure. The glaciologist has radar and seismic sounding for depth determinations and complex laboratory tests to examine ice-cores, and to discover the behaviour of ice under changing temperatures and pressures. The cartographer possesses instruments of almost unimaginable precision; he times the passage of light to measure distance, and his eyes have the range and vision of satellites and aerial cameras of extraordinary resolution, producing overlapping mosaics and stereoscopic relief. Much of the work in all these sciences is still arduous, uncomfortable and dangerous. It often seems as though the gods and demons of uncreated antarctic myths await the unwary modern explorer behind his façades of insulation, speed, electronics and mechanics.

Whatever else the future holds for the world at large and for claimants to antarctic territory in particular, may it remain a vast international laboratory for the study of geophysics, whose language is universal and whose achievements are a common heritage of humanity.

First approach to the Prince Charles Mountains.

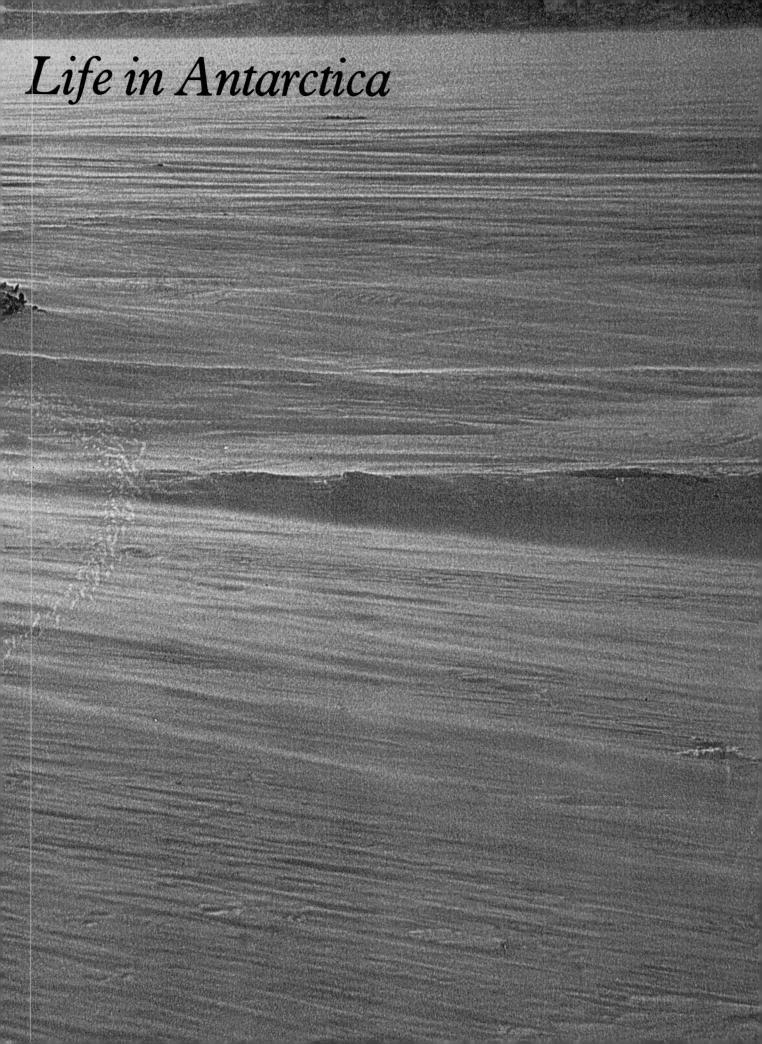

Life in Antarctica

We have considered Antarctica as a huge bi-lobate mass weighed down by millions of cubic kilometres of ice. An attempt has been made to understand the movements of ice and air. Through long-distance glasses we have scanned the course of south polar history. Now we may examine some aspects in detail and perhaps linger where there is much direct appeal. Some of the gross aspects with which the human senses are capable of dealing, we have considered, with the invisible forces of terrestrial magnetism and their moving focus in Antarctica. We have discussed one of the most beautiful and dramatic phenomena on earth, the aurora, and other, perhaps less essentially polar, occurrences which nevertheless, are amongst the main objects of human interest in high latitudes.

It would be an incomplete account without description and discussion of the animals of the south, both those which, from ancient times, have pursued their finely balanced cycles—from long before any man thought of Antarctica—and man himself, whose pres-

Elephant seal pups, known as 'porkies', on a Heard Island beach. At birth an elephant seal may weigh thirty-six kilograms; his weight will be quadrupled by the time he is weaned at the end of the summer.

ence has changed the balance, perhaps irreversibly. Today, the conscience of man is troubled that certain species, of whales especially, have been brought close to extinction, and he fears his ineptitude may have placed in jeopardy resources of inestimable material and spiritual value. For the present we will consider general aspects of antarctic life, including that of man; later there will be summary discussion of the physical resources of the south, both animal and mineral, and their exploitation and conservation.

Each age has its reasons for exploration; they and the ideals of the age change in composition even when they contain the same elements. The years bring new methods, new equipment, new ideals and new values. These are all projections from the restless mind of man; they are not part of the antarctic matrix; they provide the incentive and the implements which prise out its riches, both scientific and substantial.

I have mentioned the Eskimo proverb, 'Weather and Ice are kings'. It is a brilliant folk-saying, combining truth and imagination with economy of words. But not many people ever experience such regal weather, which may blast and freeze and kill, over-riding plans and

Young bulls. Many young and vigorous bull elephant seals contest for places on the beaches. The strongest eventually become 'beachmasters' dominating their harems of cows.

Proud birds: An emperor chick from an egg incubated on its parents' feet and nourished through late winter, is admired by them in springtime sunshine. [J.W.]

ventures, blotting out the world with furious grey blizzard, or which may be gracious and benign, capricious like the old Norse gods. Few have seen the majesty of flashing icebergs, or the endless white plain of the frozen sea that surrounds a land of perpetual glaciers. Here there is beauty, but it may be accepted only with its perils and chances—the moving iceberg driving on with inconceivable power; the shadowy, uncertain depths of crevasses; the clashing floes and the pressure of pack ice which can still make toys of man's stout ships. 'Weather and Ice are kings!'—in the Antarctic this has the same meaning as it had for the Eskimos of the northern polar twilight.

How does man live in this environment? The important thing of course is not to keep the cold out, but to keep the heat in! No matter how thick or well-insulated walls may be, they create no warmth. Without a stove the finest building in the Antarctic would be cold as a tomb; without the heat generated by a human body, eiderdowns and windproofs would be of no more value than feathers on a dead bird.

The warmth which allows life to continue is always tending to escape into the atmosphere. To understand the principles of conserving heat, it is important to remember that it is dissipated in three ways. The first is by being conducted away through a material, as heat from the end of a poker that is in the fire is transmitted to the handle. The second is by radiation through space, as the heat of the sun reaches our skins even when the air is at a temperature below freezing point. And the third is by convection—the transfer of heat in a fluid like air or water from the hotter region to the colder—as air and smoke go up the chimney, or heated water rises to a storage tank in the rafters.

One of the very best insulators—that is, one of the poorest conductors of heat—is dry air. A carefully sealed wall-panel, with horizontal partitions to prevent convection, is a better insulator filled with air than an equal thickness of solid wood. To prevent the development of convection currents and for added strength there are numerous porous materials holding air imprisoned in small pockets; these include foamed plastics, rather like pumice in texture, and glass or mineral wools. As for man, so for the other animals. Fur and feathers hold warm air entrapped, not to keep the cold out, but to prevent the escape of heat; while blubber or fat is, no less than stored nourishment, additional insulation clothing the vital deep temperature of the body.

Although the conduction of heat and its convection by air currents must be taken into account, radiation is usually the dominant cause of heat loss. Frequently, therefore, surfaces are silvered to reflect back into buildings the infra-red heat rays. External walls may be of polished metal for the same reason. The principle is well exemplified where a highly polished container—a vacuum flask or silver jug—keeps water hot for long periods, holding its temperature by internal reflection and external emission of minimum radiant heat. Some very successful insulation has been achieved by constructing walls with several sealed layers of air, horizontally partitioned against convection, and separated vertically by thin sheets of brightly polished metal foil.

Ventilation is one of the great necessities, and poses considerable problems, for buildings, and even tents, in the Antarctic. The danger of foul air, carbon monoxide poisoning or anoxia is equal to that of fire, probably, with so much tinder dry, the most constant dread of all. Wherever fresh air enters a hut or tent, in times of blizzard drift snow may be carried with it, and, if this snow be melted by the heat of the hut, it may flow back, freeze, accumulate and seal the air inlet. The price of comfort and safety is watchfulness. Most Antarcticans, sooner or later, experience the shock of fire and CO poisoning. They are fortunate if the danger is arrested without serious loss or tragedy. During the last few decades several antarctic bases have suffered the horror of fire with loss of life and with desperate consequences to the men left bereft and isolated. Fuel for the burning is inevitably on hand in so dry a climate; the conventional means of combatting fire—liquid water—may be in impossibly short supply. I was present at 'the great fire of Mawson',[74] when an unsuspected reservoir of fuel oil that had been accumulating unseen and unknown for several years in the loose rock-fill below the concrete floor caught fire and spread voraciously. No firefighting appliances on the station—and there were many—could contain the fire. After exhausting our large supplies of all extinguishers, including those producing foam and CO_2, a final desperate effort was with chains of buckets of seawater, carried, from a hole in the ice of the harbour, up ramps of snow to the roof. The building blew up shortly after the last firefighter was called down. Molten brass and aluminium ran down the rocks, while large snowdrifts remained unmelted, reflecting the heat back into the inferno.

Carbon monoxide poisoning may occur in unexpected circumstances. On one occasion during a severe antarctic blizzard, I recall, an aircraft hangar—usually a very draughty building—became hermetically sealed by snow during some routine engine testing. Three men were affected before the danger was realized, fortunately in time to sledge them to treatment and eventual recovery. A strange case of anoxia in an excavated ice-cave on Heard Island so dulled the senses of a sheltering party, including myself, that we watched candles guttering and going out, and a stove spluttering and failing, and even tried to rekindle them, before we realized the trouble, and clawed desperately through the snow-sealed entrance to gulp air and blizzard drift.

Clothing is designed on much the same principles as apply to buildings, as far as insulation is concerned. Air must be held close to the body. Foundation garments are singlets of thick but soft mesh, knitted loosely to leave maximum air-spaces; and soft, loose underpants. The air that is warmed by the body remains held in position within the cells of the mesh. Soft woollen clothes hold further air and provide ventilation. Outside everything is worn a windproof parka or anorak to prevent the cold air driving through and disturbing the cushions of warm air within, and creating wind-chill. Reflecting surfaces on clothing—as used by astro-

The relief ship, Thala Dan, *in Mawson Harbour. The formation of new ice retards the unloading of the ship.*

Fire constitutes one of the gravest dangers on an antarctic station. In 1959 this fire devastated the main engine-room at Mawson station.

Antarctic appendicectomy.

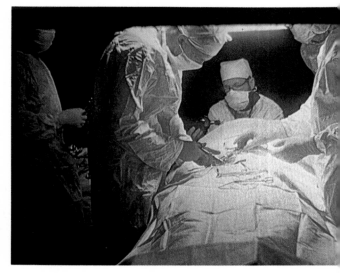

nauts and firefighters—have been tested in the Antarctic, though external garments are usually brightly coloured for distant identification. On the feet are worn lambswool inner boots over two or three pairs of thick, soft socks, then insoles of spongy plastic and outer boots of canvas, leather and rubber, containing no nails to conduct away the warmth of the feet.

At times, considerable perspiration must occur, even in Antarctica. As the warmed and humid air gradually escapes outwards from the body, it reaches a layer where frost is formed. It's common experience, at night in a tent, to strip off windproofs and outer woollens, and find a layer of white, glistering hoar. Below insoles, too, as often as not, boots may be full of it. Another type of footwear provides double rubber walls impermeable by moisture and separated by air held in soft, foamed plastic, synthetic wool or other suitable medium. On this 'vapour barrier' principle have been evolved the lightest, highly insulated boots for really low temperatures. They possess the disadvantage of all hermetically sealed garments, the trapping of moisture on the skin itself. Still, by most people, damp warmth is preferable to dry cold, and it is less dangerous. The minimum of socks required are quickly dried and changed as opportunities permit. Men travelling in aircraft and tractors, or standing for long periods of observation in intense cold, are enthusiastic about the vapour barrier boot.

I have mentioned drift snow many times. Antarctic drift, fine and dry as talcum powder, clouds the air so evenly that its streaming movement is invisible even when gusts suddenly increase its density. There is no appearance of flying flakes, just an ebb and flow of shadow. Drift snow is extraordinarily penetrating, finding a way through the smallest crack in a hut or vehicle. I have heard men softly cursing as they pursued some minute hole that was letting in buckets of drift, speaking such as men might while hunting lice in the desert —and suddenly ejaculating in triumph as though they had conquered a little living beast.

Of course, man is an interloper in Antarctica and, as such, he must expect some inconvenience. Nature

Weddell seal on sea-ice.

The US base at McMurdo Sound, Ross Island.

decreed millions of years ago that all living things depart from the Antarctic—depart or perish, or else adapt themselves to the least hospitable, least compromising environment on earth. Vegetable life on incoming continents mostly perished, and left only residual fossils of broad leaves and massive trunks, or retained a lowly lichened grip on coastal rocks, suspending all growth except for a few weeks in summer. Much the same happened with the animals, though many lowly forms of life adapted themselves to changing conditions, or evolved a specialized existence below the ice in sub-zero salt water; a few higher animals, so the evidence seems to say, changed their forms and habits to a remarkable degree, through a million generations, to enable them to cope with more and more marginal conditions, and to prey on the multitudinous oceanic hordes. And versatile man became the most successful animal of all, being able to adapt himself to any habitat at will.

Evolution is a most convenient and disturbing concept in our philosophy. It is convenient to say that penguins gave up flight through air in some tertiary paradise before any faint approach to human thought existed; that they evolved flippers and streamlined bodies to fly through water at incredible speed, and evade cruel leopard seals, whose own dim ancestors with legs, earthbound in early Eden, would have constituted a lesser foe for birds. But, however perfect the theory, the necessary natural selection, equated with infinite time and chance and mutation, is difficult to

conceive. Yet one must accept the fact that emperor penguins, for instance, as we know them, could never have migrated through tropical seas, just as they may now never travel far from the coasts of ice. They must therefore have evolved through the slow infinity of change that gave Antarctica its character. They are as much proof of change as the fossilized Glossopteris leaf or the labyrinthodont[75] at the Permian end of the time-scale.

With a solitary exception all the higher animals have become seasonal visitors, retreating to the open sea, the edge of the ice or more temperate lands for the long months of winter, and returning only for the brief silver summer. The exception is the Weddell seal, who lives through the winter in the warmer waters below the sea-ice—his warmth being entirely relative to above-ice temperatures. But he pays a hard price for his daring. Being a mammal he must breathe air, so, throughout the many months when the sea is frozen and the air too cold for him to emerge with impunity, he must keep breathing holes open in the thick sea ice, or suffocate by drowning. This he does by constantly biting and rasping the edges of his hatchway to the bitter world. And when he grows too old or his teeth are worn too low, he dies.

There are several other seals in antarctic waters, some preferring the sub-antarctic islands or the pack ice for breeding, but all, at least seasonally, visiting the continent. The ponderous elephant seal is especially common at islands such as Heard, Macquarie and South Georgia; it appears to be completely at home in its muddy wallows on the Îles de Kerguelen. The bull of this species may attain a weight of several tonnes and a length of five metres. He is a harem lord, preferring the beaches of the cold desert islands, where he may attract a hundred wives. Their pups at birth may weigh thirty-six kilograms, and by the time they are weaned

Under the ice-shelf. Below the floating shelf and the ice of the frozen winter sea, penguins and most seals do not venture. Only the remarkable Weddell seal, which keeps open a series of breathing holes through the sea-ice, and the nototheniid fishes, find sustenance under the ice. At the bottom of the drawing is a sectional view of the ice-sheet, first overlying land, then extruded as shelf-ice floating out to sea above the continental shelf, and breaking up as icebergs.

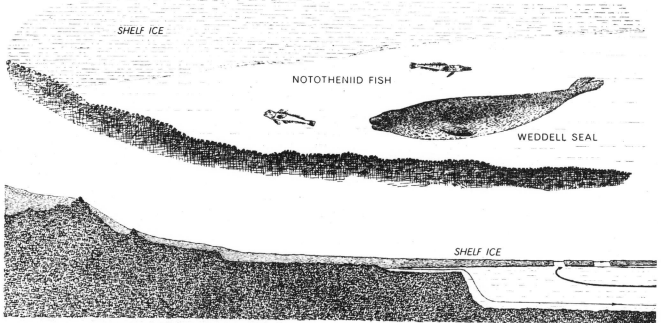

SHELF ICE

NOTOTHENIID FISH

WEDDELL SEAL

SHELF ICE

From 'The Oceanic Life of the Antarctic' by Robert Cushman Murphy. Copyright © September 1962 by Scientific American, Inc. All rights reserved.

of mother's milk they may reach more than two hundred kilograms.

On the same beaches may be observed the silver-grey and spotted leopard seals, or sea-leopards, sleek carnivorous monsters whose diet is largely composed of the gentoo and rockhopper penguins of sub-antarctic latitudes. they range these seas for food and lie up in considerable numbers on desolate beaches—such as the black volcanic sands of Heard Island—perhaps to rest from the eternally turbulent sea, but they bear their young amongst the ice-floes farther south.

The seals (Pinnipedia) may be divided into two great families—the true or earless seals (Phocidae) and the eared seals (Otariidae). The former do not use their limbs in any way as legs, progressing on shore or on ice by convulsive wave-like movements of the body; the latter may use their flippers as legs, virtually walking upon them, and on shore the hind limbs are turned forwards like feet. The Phocidae are represented in the Antarctic by the Weddell, crabeater, leopard, Ross, and elephant seals. The last-named has always been considered more a sub-antarctic than a truly antarctic species, but its prevalence along certain favourable

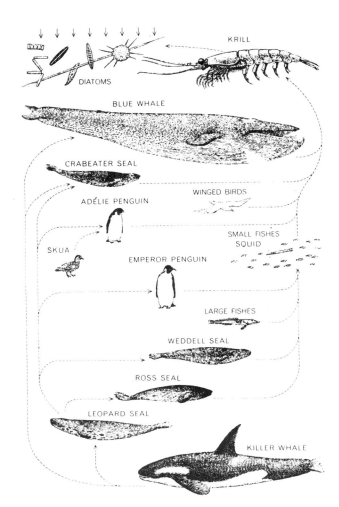

Food cycle of the marine animals is based on the krill Euphausia superba. *This crustacean feeds on diatoms: microscopic marine plants that utilize the energy of the sun (short arrows) to transform nutrients in the water into living tissue. The krill is in turn the food of whales, penguins and other birds, the crabeater seal, squids and fishes. In addition to this basic cycle there is predation by seals, penguins and large fishes on squids and small fishes; leopard seal preys on penguins and other seals and the skua eats penguin eggs and chicks.*

Attempts to brand a fierce predator, a leopard seal, are not uncontested. Insufficient is known of this carnivorous species.

The rare Ross seal. Note the striated throat and the dilated nostrils which may be completely sealed under water.

95

rocky coasts, such as of the Vestfold Hills area of the mainland, makes it appear that ice rather than a high latitude is disliked by the big elephants. However, the elephant seal differs from the other antarctic Phocidae in seldom being solitary or favouring small groups. All seals are polygamous but in this respect the elephant outclasses them all.

The southern fur seal is still comparatively rare, never having fully recovered from the ruthless depredations of the nineteenth century. It is the only eared seal that was of commercial importance in southern waters. Fanning (1832) claimed that more than a hundred thousand fur seals were slaughtered in a single year (1800) in South Georgia alone, and Biscoe estimated that about a million and a quarter skins had been taken from the same island in the half-century ending in 1825 (that is, since Cook's voyages). Possibly every colony was virtually exterminated. In the latter part of the nineteenth century it seemed that the species might

become extinct; it may now possess, in all, a population still less than twenty thousand in number. The fur seal is not a large animal, adults seldom exceeding 183 centimetres in length. The fur of the adults varies somewhat in colour but may be a very warm brown or a rich fawn. A few specimens are now seen regularly on most of the sub-antarctic islands.

The southern sea-lion, the South Australian sea-lion, Hooker's sea-lion, and probably other related species are also eared, but their pelts are coarse and were never valuable. Their yield of oil never approached that of the elephant seal.

One of the rarer true, or earless, seals of the Antarctic is that named after Ross. It is short and fat with a striated throat which expands quite grotesquely. Several times I have encountered the species: once on Heard Island where a juvenile came ashore and lingered for a day, allowing himself to be photographed from all angles; once on a large ice-floe in Prydz Bay (antarctic mainland, 75°E.) and occasionally at sea in pack ice. Particularly noticeable features of the rather frog-like head are the broad, flared nostrils which may be closed so tightly as to appear invisible.

The crabeater seal is the most abundant of all, but it is mainly to be found in the rather uncomfortable vicinity of the pack ice edge. Frequently the crabeater shows terrible scars from his close encounters with the killer whale; they are almost diagnostic of the species. It has been exploited for its skin and blubber, about fifty thousand adult animals being taken from the northern Weddell Sea in the 1892–93 season. The later sealers always had a major interest in blubber and oil and, ultimately, the industry based on these largely supplanted that based on fur. On Heard Island, at the time of the *Challenger* expedition (1874–75), there were

Sheathbills, the only land birds on Heard Island.

Wandering albatross on nest, Kerguelen, in southern Indian Ocean.

Skuas as scavengers, Heard Island.

Typical vegetation of sub-antarctic islands: cushion plants, grasses and 'Kerguelen cabbage', said to be an antiscorbutic.

Massive kelp writhes between the rocks along the coast of Macquarie Island.

97

still forty sealers scattered in parties along the coast, rendering down the blubber of elephant seals, but by then the greater days of all sealing were over. I often used to come upon the remains of great iron try-pots, relics of the old oil-renderers, rusted and half buried in the sands and cushion-plants of the beaches and headlands of Heard, Macquarie and the Kerguelen Islands.

All seals, at some time or another, haul themselves out of the sea and rest or breed on land or ice. The whales (Cetacea) are completely marine and therefore, perhaps, do not usually enter into accounts of Antarctica as much as do the seals and penguins. But, on the other hand, they have been the greatest magnet of all attracting men to the antarctic regions and, to date, their exploitation has brought great material return to man. Whales and seals have been hunted for at least a thousand years for their flesh and their oil, the latter having been used for lighting, heating and lubrication, and for the treatment of wool and leathers since very early times. Whale oil has been commonly employed as an additive to mineral oils, but in many of its older uses it has been supplanted by oils refined from those of the wells, by other fuels or by electricity. The chemical hydrogenation of whale oil enabled it to be used for both margarine and soap, and for innumerable other derivatives. Every part of the whale was utilized in the end, much of it, directly or indirectly, for human consumption as food or medicine; even the percentage of flesh and bone converted to fertilizers meant an increase in the food yield of the world. It may seem strange that, now, with the suddenness that was inevitable, the hunting of whales must be expressed mainly in the past tense. Mankind takes stock, and his evaluation no longer only concerns wealth that may be sold: Leviathan cannot be bought.

The great whales: the blue whale (top), with a mean length of twenty-four metres and a mean weight of eighty-four tonnes, is thought to be the largest animal that has ever existed on earth; the humpback and fin whales are drawn in proportion; they average, respectively, thirty-three and fifty tonnes. Other baleen whales (Mysticeti) are smaller, the sei and minke averaging, respectively, thirteen and seven tonnes.
The killer whale depicted hunting a seal, is of the toothed (Odontoceti) group which includes the sperm whale (averaging thirty-five tonnes) and the dolphins and porpoises.

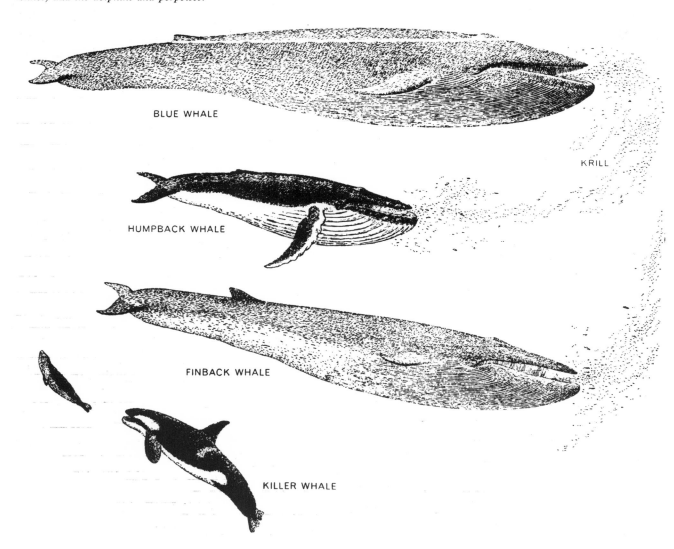

BLUE WHALE

KRILL

HUMPBACK WHALE

FINBACK WHALE

KILLER WHALE

From the apical viewpoint of the mammal man, the mammal whale is amongst the most efficient food-producers. Whales do naturally what man may eventually be forced to attempt synthetically; that is, they produce food from its elements. In fact, they make use of intermediate stages—plant and animal plankton, which successively convert in the light of the sun the nutrient chemical resources of the sea into the bulk of living bodies. Some whales—the baleen species (of the order Mysticeti)—take the minute plankton directly as food; others—of the toothed species (Odontoceti), which include relatively small members such as dolphins and porpoises, feed upon fish and squid and higher forms of life, as do the seals and seabirds.

Round the antarctic coasts, for an average distance of perhaps fifteen hundred kilometres, anyway as far as the Antarctic Convergence, there is a closed cycle of planktonic life depending on many factors, including the arrival from the north of rich deep currents which deposit vast quantities of organic matter, the marked seasonal changes, and a lower salinity (than that of lower latitudes). It is a complex cycle; in effect, it ensures that antarctic seas are rich in the nutrients required for incalculable numbers of minute plant plankton which, in turn, provide assimilable food for animal life. The existence of the zooplankton, the

Blue-eyed shags, a sub-antarctic species of cormorant found on several of the lonely 'albatross' islands.

Killer whale. (H. G. Ponting, B.A.E., 1910–13)

Sei whale near Wilkes Land. [A.C.-D.]

smallest kinds of shrimp-like and other animals, provides the answer to the old wonderment, 'Master, I marvel how the fishes live in the sea.' It is an answer that differs little from that of the sage, 'Why, as men do a-land . . . the great ones eat up the little ones'! This is more than a mere proverb; it is a succinct statement concerning the cycle of life (but, of course, it is metaphorical in that no cetacean is a fish!).

Plankton, by derivation and definition, connotes those forms of life which are moved by the ocean's currents, which drift within its surface or submarine cycles. It includes not only the microscopic organisms but larger

creatures with a limited power of adaptation to variations in salinity and temperature. If, in fact, the organisms drift beyond their climatic zones they die and eventually revert to their constituent substances.

The high concentration of plankton or secondary forms of life in antarctic waters attracts whales and seals which, for protection from the intense cold, have developed enormous thicknesses of fatty blubber beneath the skin. This blubber is also a surplus food store, especially for use during breeding excursions to warmer zones. For man, it yielded the valuable oil; averaging something over ten tonnes per beast. All whale species move towards convenient summer latitudes or con-

Brooding black-browed albatross.

Black-browed albatross on pedestal nest, reinhabited each year.

Black-browed albatross chicks on ancestral nests, Heard Island.

ditions to bear their young. The precise life histories of all economic species have now been under study for a long period; the basic life of the minutiae of the southern oceans has been investigated much more recently. In sum, all the facts are sufficiently well known now, to enable the whaling industry, if ever it may be revived, to be pursued intelligently, with a view to conservation of all species. Unfortunately knowledge is not enough; for years after the whaling nations could foresee the dearth of the great species they continued the industry, and still sectional interests continue to operate in a realm where there never has been, and perhaps never can be, absolute, international jurisdiction.

Of the toothed Odontoceti, the principal whale of commerce is the sperm whale, which dives deeply, feeds mainly on squid, and roves the world; of the Mysticeti—the baleen group—the principal members are the humpback, fin, sei, and blue whales, the last being the largest, reaching up to thirty metres in length. Instead of teeth, the 'baleen' species possess sieve-curtains of the flexible material (baleen) which was the old 'whalebone' of commerce, of greatest value before the age of synthetic plastics.

The dolphins of the toothed species include the ferocious killer whale, seven to nine metres long, a truly carnivorous animal which attacks, in schools, some of his cetacean relations as well as the seals. An extensive literature asserts that the killers have consolidated as an instinct the habit of up-ending ice-floes on which seals are at rest; they would doubtless be indiscriminate if they upset an odd hunter or antarctic explorer.[76] Another of the beasts' unpleasant habits is said to be the breaking of floes from beneath, to investigate prom-

ising shadows. Shackleton and his team were not a little afraid of this happening while they were drifting on the ice of the Weddell Sea in 1915.

The other evident 'killer' of the Antarctic, the much smaller leopard seal, may restrict his diet mainly to penguins. He does not attack anything when he is out of the water. Many times I have watched penguins strolling unconcernedly within easy reach of the evil-looking tight mouths of leopards, and I myself have walked amongst them without their evincing the slightest appetitive interest. In water this seal is in an entirely different element; there he is swift, sudden and ruthless death to penguins. He patrols just outside the breakers, often as not, of a beach where penguins land—and the wash of the sea is filled with the skins of the birds.

Light-mantled sooty albatrosses on the cliffs of Macquarie Island.

Light-mantled sooty albatross chick, Heard Island.

101

One of the greatest species of commerce, the famous right whale, was relentlessly hunted for centuries in the north, gradually being harried to his most distant retreats. He was easier to catch than most whales, being a slower swimmer. Both baleen and oil were plentiful and of good quality. The same sort of exploitation as the fur seals suffered eventually brought the creature to near extinction, and, by a reasonable measure of international agreement, it is now protected.

Gradually, new techniques and knowledge made it possible to kill the faster, deeper-diving whales. Weapons of great power and accuracy, merciless and cruel, were invented to replace the old harpoon; into the vast, defenceless animals were shot explosive barbed arrows. The dead or dying whales were inflated to prevent their sinking. Small shore-based vessels, rowed by intrepid men, were replaced by fast, powerful diesel-engined chasers of several hundred tonnes, and, instead of the flensing stations on the grey sub-antarctic isles where the whales were cut up and the blubber rendered, large factory ships took these operations thousands of kilometres from land. Stern ramps and tackle capable of hauling whales bodily from the sea speeded all processes. Each factory ship might have a fleet of up to a dozen chasers and, as late as the middle century, there might be up to thirty factory ships with their

satellites ranging the oceans outside the pack. In older days, whales were out of range if they were much more than a hundred kilometres from the shore-based stations, either on islands like South Georgia, or on coasts—such as that of Western Australia—close to their migration routes for breeding. From the beginning the new pattern of factory ships, specially built and designed for their purpose, threatened the whales' survival. As many as forty thousand whales were captured in antarctic waters in a single year; in the mid-century years, the total world catch might be sixty thousand yearly.

When the great factory ships first cruised the open antarctic seas, the most commonly hunted whales were the blue and the fin, the former being preferred because of its size. In the 1930s there was a peak year when thirty thousand blue whales and ten thousand fin whales were slaughtered. The blue whale catch was halved within a decade, for no other reason than that they were not there to be caught. In the same period there was a concomitant rise in the number of fin whales taken and, just before the war, there was a peak in numbers, equalling that of the blue whales ten years

Juvenile Dominican gull, with sheathbills, Heard Island.

Giant petrel. The largest of the petrels, this sub-antarctic and antarctic species, like the albatrosses is circumpolar in distribution.

King penguins, the sub-antarctic cousins of the emperors, largest of all penguin species.

earlier. After the Second World War, the whaling factory ships pursued their quarry with new vigour. Norwegian, British, USSR, US and Japanese fleets ranged the southern oceans, insatiable in their search. It was even then evident that the blue whale population had not recovered from the pre-war onslaught. Year by year, the numbers caught, even those sanctioned by the International Whaling Commission—a United Nations authority—fell lower and lower. By the mid-'sixties there were no blue whales caught. For two decades the fin whale catch was sustained in numbers, making the costly factory fleets economically viable; catches usually numbered twenty or twenty-five thousand annually. It

The edge of the pack ice. Food is usually available amongst the upturned floes at the edge of the pack, attracting not only the primary krill feeders, such as penguins, terns, petrels and the crabeater seals depicted, but their predators, the roving leopard seals and killer whales. Note that, as with icebergs, only a small fraction of the pack ice floats above the surface.

seemed that perhaps 'Maximum Sustainable Yields' might be acceptable. But, again, there occurred the recurrent tragedy. The fins became scarce and, by the 'seventies, they were as rare as the blues. The smaller sei whales, scarcely hunted at all until after the war, gradually became acceptable, but they, too, declined in numbers. The prodigal century approaches its end without a single species, other than the small minke—a twelfth the weight of the great blue whale—and the ubiquitous sperm whale being commercially hunted. Many nations have abandoned the pelagic industry and withdrawn from commercial whaling; those which continue, including the USSR and Japan principally, take about a tenth between them of what were once available.[77]

All over the world, biologists and conservationists continue to cry for a halt to the whaling industry, many of whose products are now synthesized by other means. Their voice has doubtless had its effect; there is a new

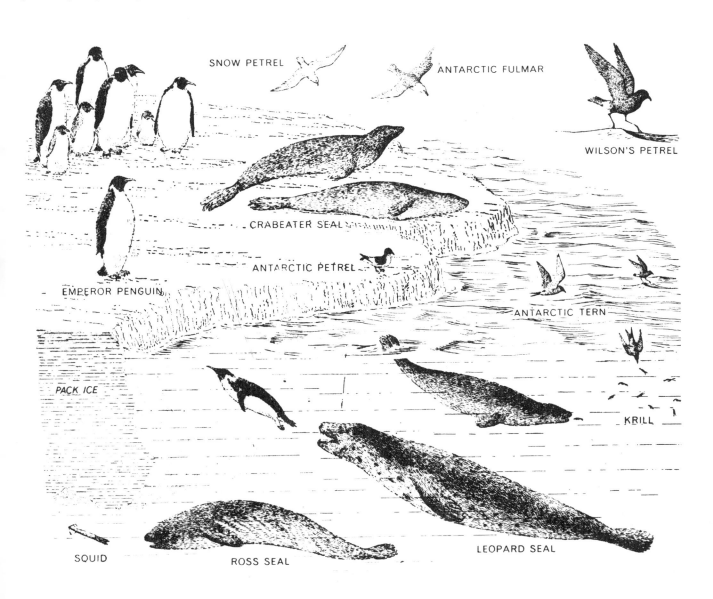

SNOW PETREL
ANTARCTIC FULMAR
WILSON'S PETREL
CRABEATER SEAL
ANTARCTIC PETREL
EMPEROR PENGUIN
ANTARCTIC TERN
PACK ICE
KRILL
SQUID
ROSS SEAL
LEOPARD SEAL

Emperor penguins, Cape Crozier, Ross Island.

Emperor penguin rookery in spring. [M.C.]

Tobogganing emperor penguins, showing their usual means of travel over sea-ice, propelling themselves by feet and flippers.

The track in new snow of a tobogganing emperor penguin moving over sea-ice.

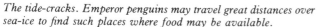

The tide-cracks. Emperor penguins may travel great distances over sea-ice to find such places where food may be available.

and hopeful realization that our civilization must recognize the sanctity of species and habitat. The sadness of the matter, however, in the antarctic seas, is that only the fact of immense scarcity of whales, and the consequent lack of commercial return from major whaling operations, really give the residue a tenuous hope of survival. If that should become assured, perhaps the recovery will be matched by greater human wisdom, compassion and knowledge of the integrity of all life.

It is certain that the biological and oceanographical studies of southern waters will continue, with a focus upon the altered balance of the totally interrelated species. The fundamental krill have greatly increased in numbers with the demise of so large a proportion of the antarctic whales. This increase has led, without doubt, to changes in the numbers of its others predators—seals, seabirds, fish and other marine life. Should not man also be listed? Krill have been trawled for human consumption by the USSR, Japan, and the Federal Republic of Germany; other nations are deeply interested in krill, scale-fish and squid, all with potentials of millions of tonnes as contribution to the human food chain. However, great concern is expressed by scientists that changes in the krill ecosystem may not be reversible. Again it seems that man may change the balance of the oceanic food-cycle and, in doing so, exclude, as surely as death by explosive harpoon, the recovery in life status of the great whales.

Major projects in oceanography and marine biology since the famous voyage of the *Challenger*, by the British Research Expeditions of the *Discovery II* in the 1930s and 1940s, by the vessels of all nations participating in the IGY, but, especially, by the USSR *Ob* and the US National Science Foundation's vessel, *Eltanin*, have led to the great continuing international study of BIOMASS mentioned earlier, emanating from the USA and from the British Institute of Oceanographic Sciences. There is international concern: the Scientific Committee of Antarctic Research, the Scientific Committee on Ocean Research, the Food and Agriculture

Organization (of the United Nations), as well as the International Whaling Commission, and the Inter-governmental Oceanographic Commission, are all giving the BIOMASS[76] research programme their support. It is likely to occupy more than what is left of the twentieth century.

This section will be concluded with an account of life above the ice, and I will briefly recapitulate concerning man and his machines, and his vanishing dog teams, before considering the highly specialized and beautiful birds of the far south.

We have considered how man lives in Antarctica; how he conserves warmth. It is possible to warm and insulate huts and cabins so that their occupants can feel literally at home in controlled conditions of temperature and humidity. Often the difference of temperature inside and outside a hut will exceed 50° or 60°C. Generally huts are provided with uninsulated porches in which people may gain shelter from wind and drift, remove outer garments, and hang them with snow in their folds; it will remain unthawed and dry. Straw whisks or brushes are always provided for the removal of dust-like snow, but if men are going in and out of huts during a blizzard they will often leave clothes unbrushed in the porch until they require them again. Except for cost and inconvenience, there are no bars to men and women living comfortably in the world's most rigorous climate.

Away from base there may be calm sunny weather when the snow reflects the benign sun, but people must never be far from the outer clothing they may certainly require at short notice. They may be travelling on foot, with dogs, in tractors with sledge caravans, or by

aircraft. While engines are running it is possible to channel warmth back into the cabin. It is usual, now, with major inland traverses, for a 'power-pack' sledge to be included in the tractor train; this has generators

Nesting cape pigeons. These birds are petrels, and the study shows the characteristic upper mandible.

Cape pigeons afloat; antarctic terns in flight, at Heard island.

for all purposes, including the heating of sledge caravans and for welding equipment to cope with fractured metal.

In tents, however, while a meal is being prepared, the heat of a pressure stove is welcome. Ventilation, of course, is a problem with any enclosed space, particularly if the air is filled with flying drift.

Well garbed, a man may be sufficiently comfortable in temperatures as low as $-30°$ or $-40°C$, provided he is protected from the wind. A tent, well pitched and anchored with sufficient snow or *névé* blocks, is at least as comfortable to sleep in as a modern vehicle. Sleeping bags are insulated from the hard and cold surface by mattresses of sponge rubber or quilted blocks of foamed plastic. People gradually become adept at performing all sorts of tasks in heavy gloves, removing the outer mitts only when a quality of special precision is essential.

Subantarctic islands: it is essentially for breeding that sea-birds, such as albatrosses, petrels and skuas, throng the small islands of the far south. The larger petrels, terns and albatrosses nest in the open; cliff prions, cape pigeons and other small petrels use rock crannies or construct burrows.

Of course, pitching and striking tents takes time, especially in wind and drift. Often a motor vehicle, towing sledges and caravans, can take advantage of brief lulls in the weather and proceed over valuable kilometres when there would be insufficient time, and possibly resolution, to break camp. In modern antarctic projects mechanized transport is inevitable. Men and supplies put down by plane may enable a maximum number of precious summer days to be spent in far inland areas. There are still problems of lubricants and engine operation on the high, cold plateau. However, the solution of all such difficulties is well within the capacity of our technology. Should the reasons exist for cities in the Antarctic, cities there will be, and, though the conditions of blizzard and cold may be of longer duration, and more rigorous, life in those cities will be as safe, organized and comfortable as in their northern hemisphere counterparts. The problems of terrain are less simply solved.

American engineers, during the IGY, constructed a safe 'road', more than a thousand kilometres long, from Little America to their inland station Byrd (lat. 80°S., long. 120°W.) by blasting, bulldozing and filling in

CAPE PIGEON

BLUE-EYED SHAG

GIANT FULMAR

STORM PETREL

WHALE BIRD

107

crevasses. On the plateau, ice may be regarded as a white rock to be hewn or crushed and used in building or roadmaking. It is not, of course, feasible to build such roads while exploring new territory and, unfortunately, in mountainous areas crevasses are often so common as to make the use of tractors and other vehicles hazardous. In the Prince Charles Mountains, south of Mawson, my vehicles came upon dangerous crevassing some kilometres from the nearest exposed rock.

Sledge dogs have long been bred in the arctic countries of the far north, and those in Antarctica, or their ancestors, were recruited from Labrador, Alaska and Greenland. Historically, they were essential; today, as we have seen, they may generally be replaced by mechanical 'skidoos' of various kinds. A few dog teams will perhaps survive the century, for sentimental reasons, and because they may still be very useful in difficult terrain—and they are most adept at exercising their masters. The dogs still used occasionally by Australian and New Zealand expeditions have descended from ancestors bred on Heard Island and at Mawson, from stock left in Melbourne by a French expedition returning to France soon after the last war. Since then some new blood has been admitted.

They are big dogs, huskies, weighing up to forty-five kilograms or more, and varying considerably in build and appearance, some being much rougher-coated than others. Their dense pelt gives them adequate protection from cold, and they live tranquilly in the open, provided temperatures do not rise high enough for them to become wet. They curl up in dry snow and allow themselves to be almost buried in drift. Quarrelsome amongst themselves, they are usually gentle towards their masters. Their harness is constructed from tough flexible webbing—often lamp-wick—and various kinds

Like the emperor the king penguins incubate their eggs and carry the young chicks on their horny feet.

The kings' rookery. Most colourful of all penguins, the kings, second in size only to the emperors, breed on sub-antarctic latitudes.

Young king penguins in their juvenile brown down, surrounded by their colourful parents, Kerguelen.

A pair of Adélie penguins at their stony nest.

Young Adélie penguin, soon to go to sea for the first time.

Most Adélie penguins lay two eggs but, as a rule, only one is hatched.

of traces are used to suit the terrain. Dogs in tandem —one after another on either side of a long centre-trace —possess great pulling power, but fan-traces—each dog on a separate lead—are safer in crevassed ice.

Loads have frequently averaged forty-five kilograms weight per dog on sea-ice and good plateau surfaces. Stefansson reported dog teams pulling an average of ninety kilograms per dog for a thousand kilometres in the Arctic. Dogs, flown inland to mountain areas with an expert dog-man have proved their value even in this mechanical age. Anyone who has travelled with dogs has mixed memories, but he recalls their companionship with affection, and their gallant service with gratitude.

In this kind of travelling, men are fully exposed to the weather, and for warmth they will frequently run or ski alongside or ahead of the dogs, even when loads are light, and they could ride the sledges. A man should be fit physically when sledging; he should be able, if necessary, to travel on foot as long and as far as his dogs.

Evening and morning are the busy times. In the evening those in charge of the dogs proceed with feeding, unharnessing and tethering while other men erect tents and prepare the meal. Usually at night the dogs are tired. In the morning, during the harnessing, they are lively and quarrelsome. A disagreement may develop with extraordinary suddenness and convert a well-ordered team into a howling, fighting mob, with traces tangled almost inextricably and with all dogs seemingly athirst for blood. To such difficulties may be added the whine and bewilderment of blizzard, when the world is lost and you are blindfolded by swirling, cubic whiteness.

Man shares the antarctic winter with only one other living creature beside the dog—the emperor penguin. I shall always associate dog and penguin, for it was at the end of a long August journey with dogs, over sea-ice, that I first visited a rookery of the immense birds. For a day or two before reaching the main congregation (at the Taylor Glacier, long. 61°E.) we encountered solitary birds. I recall my first sight of a group of emperors promenading by a pressure crack in the ice. Nine huge birds provided a strange display, unlike any other manifestation of bird behaviour. They strutted and bowed and stood in statuesque groups ignoring our presence. We were on the fringe of emperor penguin territory, the domain of tall, proud birds which survive more fearful conditions than any other creatures on earth.

Even in the dull light of the overcast and snowing sky, their pale, creamy-yellow breasts shone like satin, and the vivid chrome patches on both sides of their heads were brighter than anything else in Antarctica except the sunset sky. The big birds had black, expressionless eyes and carbon black heads which absorbed all light, so that they seemed almost two-dimensional, except for the curved streaks of their purple-pink bills. They waddled along in a comical yet tremendously dignified fashion, lifting their heads from time to time to utter an extraordinarily penetrating, resonant cry like

Predators. Always cruising round the coasts of subantarctic islands, and at the edge of the pack ice, is the carnivorous leopard seal whose diet is anything he can get, but mainly penguins. Adélies are extremely fast and evasive when pursued; their impetus may be such that they shoot out of the water a metre or more to regain the safety of the ice or the rock of their nesting islands. The skuas are watchful for any unguarded penguin eggs or chicks.

the sound of a concertina abruptly starting and, after half a second, as suddenly ending.

Just before a blizzard descended upon us we noticed individuals or small groups processing over the ice. We just managed to reach a small island. As dusk fell the weather cleared a little. Immense icebergs were grounded all around us; some revealed enormous pressure cracks from base to summit. The failing light robbed them of substance but not of size. There was a leaden stillness—with the forlorn cries of the loneliest birds in the world sounding eerily through the long subzero night.

With the size of the emperor penguin—he may weigh 31.75 kilograms[79] and stand erect at just over a metre—is bound up his whole problem of rearing a

SKUA

ADÉLIE PENGUIN

LEOPARD SEAL

From 'The Oceanic Life of the Antarctic' by Robert Cushman Murphy. Copyright © September 1962 by Scientific American, Inc. All rights reserved.

Adélie penguin rookery. Scores of thousands of Adélie penguins migrate south to the coasts of Antarctica each summer to nest at ancestral sites. Nests are of loose stones gathered and regathered through the years.

family of one solitary chick. The seasonal break-out of sea-ice occurs, as a rule, in January or February. Though, on the coast, the midsummer period of continuous daylight is then over, the open water is at its nearest to the continent. Obviously, therefore, it is the time for adolescent penguins, in fact for all young birds, to make their first acquaintance with the sea. The smaller species, such as the Adélie—the common penguin of the antarctic coasts—are able to assemble, mate and produce well-fledged youngsters within the relatively fine months of summer— from October to February. They grow at a prodigious rate, nurtured on food regurgitated by their parents. Fortunately, their increasing demands for food are generally matched by its greater availability as the ice break-up gains impetus.

The emperor chick also makes his first acquaintance with the sea in January and February. But, unlike his smaller cousins, he cannot reach near maturity in the few brief summer months; he is just too big. Neither could he grow fast enough from a 454 gram egg, nor could his parents stuff him with sufficient food. So it is that the most extraordinary breeding cycle has been evolved by the emperors.

The adults converge on their rookery sites in March or early April, swimming, or trekking over the newly frozen sea, according to season. They make good speed by lying prone on the ice and tobogganing on their breasts, propelling themselves with feet and flippers. All known rookeries are either on floating ice or on rock-based ice connected to the sea. In a period of almost a century about forty major breeding colonies have been located around the entire coast of the antarctic continent.

When the birds are assembled, there commences a period of elaborate ceremonial. The emperors promenade, bow to each other, display their magnificence and converse with cries very different from the lonely concertina calls of the sea-ice. Male and female use different forms of a similar cry. According to the findings of an expedition[80] which spent a year in Adélie Land observing the emperors, this is the only aspect of the birds' behaviour which instantly defines the sexes. The culmination of the courtship and mating is the laying of a solitary egg per couple in the month of May, about two months after the birds first muster. Consider the position! Neither bird has eaten for two months, the sea is frozen far beyond the horizon, the great penguins are brooding nestless on naked ice, and the darkness, the blizzards and extreme cold of winter are upon the coasts of Antarctica.

It is then that the females, who have treasured their eggs on their black horny feet for no more than twenty-four hours, shielding them beneath their pendulous bodies, suddenly decamp, leaving their precious eggs to the fathers. They allow them to roll gently onto the ice, then, with stately and graceful movements, they depart for distant horizons and the remote square meals they must at all costs discover. The male birds eagerly claim the eggs, placing them upon their feet and covering them with their lower breasts.

For two months father patiently incubates the egg. When blizzards are so bitter that life itself is threatened, the big birds slowly shuffle together until they rest in

A pair of McCormick skuas. These birds, the natural scavengers of the antarctic coasts, are common in the southern summer. [W.R.J.D.]

one great huddle, exposing a minimum of body area to the blast. The females return in excellent condition ready to take over the hatched chicks, to feed them with regurgitated shrimp-paste and other planktonic or fishy delicacies. Again the penguins cry, each to each, until they recognize their mates. The male bird, emaciated and dull after four months as lover, husband and father, waddles slowly away to the north. But he will return.

There is, as may be imagined, considerable infant mortality all along the line. Eggs are frozen or broken, often by an excess of solicitude; small youngsters are trampled on as the birds huddle together during a storm; parents fall to fierce predators such as leopard seals out in the northern waters and their chicks eventually starve and perish.

Late in the afternoon of the day we left the island, we sighted the actual rookery. Alongside the blue tongue of glacial ice that projected far out through the sea ice, there appeared a smudge out of tone and keeping with all the rest of the world of ice. From kilometres away we saw it as we raced over the frosty sea. And then, slowly, the smudge gained texture until it became an assembly of great standing birds, nearly all bearing on their horny feet grey chicks which peered forth with white-ringed eyes.

One of the strangest effects of all was auditory. Each chick piped with the voice of a singing bird, such as one might hear in a summer garden, only very much louder and richer. It was the sweetest natural sound I ever heard in Antarctica.

Giant petrels nest on most of the sub-antarctic islands and at some favourable continental sites.

Juvenile antarctic birds are balls of fluffy down. A skua chick.

Mating ceremonial, gentoo penguins, Macquarie Island.

There were still many months to go before the rookery would deliver its young to the sea. After another month the chicks were able to move away from their parents and form small protective huddles of their own. Their rapid growth towards summer freedom and self-sufficiency required foraging by both parents now. Over the white sea-ice there must be endless comings and goings, effort almost beyond imagination, so that a new generation may be launched in its right season.

The little Adélie penguins are known everywhere round the coasts and off-shore islands of Antarctica. Their behaviour often resembles that of the emperors, but they mate at the beginning of a summer and, as a rule, are able to rear their one or two offspring before the sea refreezes.

So often in discussing any grand theme in limited time and space, one faces the alternatives of being summary, scientific and comprehensive or of taking but a small part and endeavouring to illumine it sufficiently to cause one's listeners or readers to want to discover ways of exploring the rest for themselves. I have used both these methods in this book, and left many pictures and maps for more intensive study—and to speak for themselves. There is a third way: that of touching swiftly and lightly on many facets almost at random; this method ought to indicate that the field is vast and fascinating, and certainly worth further examination by those whose interest is stimulated. I shall make this sort of approach in completing my section on life in Antarctica. In the appendix I have listed scientific names of species mentioned, and have included an Antarctic reading list.

The staunch little Adélie penguin, known to all antarctic voyagers, is the true harbinger of the far southern summer. You may encounter him quite alone in the late spring making his way steadily over the frozen sea, the forerunner of millions that have felt the urgent call to propagate their kind, and that are following somewhere behind him over the white northern horizon. At about the same time the swift, keen-eyed skuas—the preying birds of the Antarctic—arrive by air, also in ones and twos. Both return to the harsh nesting islands and headlands of their ancestors, where, as the summer matures, there will be many hours of sun-warmed rock. How leaps the heart of the Antarctican of any nation to see the first Adélie showing faith in the possibility of a nightlong sun, and the bold skua winging in to dissipate the gloom.

However instinctive and automatic they may be, the ceremonies of the Adélies' courtship are strangely moving to the observer. Comical perhaps they are, as the rather plain little penguins promenade and raise their bumpy heads in desperate cries of hope or annunciation; human emotions are stirred pleasantly by all the apparent ceremony of the courtship and mating. But there is pathos in the way the penguins solemnly collect the loose stones used by countless generations of birds and present them to each other to make the crude stone circles which serve as nests. The stones are scattered by a year's blizzards, are frozen hard to the rocks by the salt spray, but they will be aired and sunned and rearranged in the future, times without number. It is one of the most moving atavisms in the world.

Emperor penguins comparing offspring at the end of winter. [D.P.]

The three-month-old chicks of emperor penguins take the sun at Taylor Glacier (long. 61°E.).

As a species, the Adélie suffers from two frightful dangers: that the pack ice will not break out sufficiently for food-gathering by the parents, and that the sea will refreeze before the young are ready to leave the colonies. There is ample evidence that these events occur from time to time, for the hollows and recesses of many coastal and island rookeries are dense with the bodies of almost mature chicks, dehydrated but not decomposed. It is difficult to distinguish the generations of the dead; perhaps they are separated by five or ten years, but time alters them very little. Parent birds have been observed travelling very great distances in efforts to bring food to their young, but, once in a while, 'weather and ice' are fatally tyrannous.

With many variations, penguin life continues through every southern latitude almost to the Equator. Australians, South Africans and South Americans are all familiar with their home species whose hardier cousins remained in the south. The greatest band of all seabird life lies in the middle latitudes of the forties and fifties, where islands provide nesting places—for what other reason would any bird of the sea come to dull land?—and seasons to suit the various species. I cannot describe all the sub-antarctic penguins, even of the better known islands. There are the vociferous, indignant macaronis, and their close Macquarie Island relations, the royals. Both have fine golden crests and make a splendid sight along the black rocks of a spray-swept littoral. They appear rather uppish towards the eternally surprised little rockhoppers, with their side-feathered heads decorated as though by wisps of pale yellow straw. The gentoos are quieter and more sedate; they are uncrested, but attractively flecked in maturity on the head and neck. The ring or 'chinstrap' penguin looks like its nickname, his black cap quite evidently held in position. All these more northern relatives of the Adélie resemble him in some respects; perhaps all penguins possess more obvious resemblances than differences. They all balance their lives very critically with the seasons.

The king is the brightest, sleekest and most mobile of all the penguins. He is well known in appearance, since he manages, pretty often, to survive the indignity of removal to zoological concentration camps. If ever you should see him in his glory on such places as the green, windy coastlands of Kerguelen, or the shingle beaches of Macquarie Island, you will gaze fascinated by his golden ear-patches, his blue-black cloak, and his saffron, satin breast, by his graceful movements in a serried company—and you will know that he must be only half alive in captivity.

In the summer the far south is visited by skuas, representing the gull family (Lariformes), and by several of the petrels (Procellariidae). Watchful for unguarded eggs or chicks, the McCormick skua is a fearsome predator, always wheeling round the Adélie rookeries and the burrows or nesting crannies of the petrels. No guileless or unwary bird is safe in the Antarctic; somewhere the beady eyes of the skua are watching. The little black and white storm petrels fly erratically and the snow petrels rise and fall and flutter like blown papers to avoid the arrowswift flight and attack of the skua. Life is so finely balanced along the antarctic coasts, harsh even in summer. Many times I have watched the birds constantly wheeling over the granite arms and drifting floes of Mawson harbour, often in the bright summer midnight, with all the icebergs flushed golden far out on the northern horizon.

The skua feasts from living prey or carrion and yet appears in a manner fastidious, retaining his dignity even amongst the offal of a seal. The birds are generally to be seen in pairs and they share any food either may capture. They frequently nest close to a colony of Adélie penguins, swiftly stealing whatever is left unguarded. The McCormick skua is not infrequently

Black-browed sooty albatross and young, Heard Island.

Rockhopper penguin, a tufted sub-antarctic species. [A.C.-D.]

Take-off. A light-mantled sooty albatross launches itself from the cliffs of Heard Island.

met far inland, high up on the antarctic plateau; his cousin, the southern skua, is very common in the sub-antarctic. Both find warmer winter quarters, but, generally speaking, the northern limit of the antarctic species does not coincide with the southern limit of his cousin.

Of the flying birds actually nesting on the continent, one might make particular mention of a species already briefly referred to above. This is the exquisite snow petrel, pure white except for black bill and feet, which breeds not only in coastal rock-clefts but in crannies of mountains far inland. It arrives in flocks, often flying so high in the bitter air that the birds are lost to sight. Most of the petrels find food amongst the pack ice and brash, where, as a result of waves upsetting floes, great numbers of small shrimps and other crustaceans are isolated and exposed. There is frequently, also, organic matter left undigested or rejected by the larger marine mammals.

The islands of the sub-antarctic latitudes possess a far greater wealth of bird life than the continent. Albatrosses, petrels, terns, gulls and cormorants breed on them, choosing their favourite terrain either inside or outside the Antarctic Convergence. The bird life of Kerguelen, for instance, differs markedly from that of Heard Island, only five hundred kilometres away but within the Convergence and, as a result, bearing proportionately a much greater area of permanent ice.

Like the emperor penguin, the great wandering albatross has a chick to nourish beyond a summer's kindly span, but he prefers the warmer islands. It is a never-to-be-forgotten experience to come upon a huge solitary bird brooding amongst the sparse herbage. Like all birds of the far south she displays little fear in the presence of humans, but she may rise quite composedly and spread her immense wings, two or three metres, a little in the manner adopted in her earlier courtship display, while you stand utterly astounded and fascinated. It is so different an experience from that of watching the peerless wanderer wave-skimming at sea, where she is really in her perfect element. A wandering albatross on land seems to have strayed from a Sinbad fable.

Amongst the cliff crags breed the lesser albatrosses, most species on ancestral nests which may be pedestalled by many years' accretion of mud, vegetation and guano. Few ornithologists may imagine greater delight than that of spending two or three hours on the ledges, of a high cliff-face, watching the black-brows or the light-mantled sooties sweep in from the sea and fearlessly alight alongside.

Antarctic Prospect

Over the inexorable changes of weather and ice, from season to season, century to century, in the millennia which seem to show rhythmical variations in the patterns of world glaciation, man has had no control. His statistics over the last two or three centuries, since he began grappling with problems of his environment in the northern hemisphere, show little that seems orderly or cyclical; perhaps a general decline in rainfall, possibly a return to more variable conditions, and a recession, at lower latitudes, to the hard late mediaeval winters, as those depicted by the Breughels or Hendrik Avercamp. Some scientists have considered that the apparent slight cooling of the earth has caused a 'blocking system' resulting in an accentuated latitudinal wave movement in the circumpolar west to east jet-streams[81] which, formerly stronger and more constant, have appeared latterly to bring down large masses of polar air to temperate latitudes, while providing, for the same reason, milder winters in the frigid zones.

It is certain that, in all parts of the world, there are unexpected vagaries of season providing famine or bounty, disaster or benign conditions; it is equally true that more accurate forecasting of these events would be of incalculable benefit to mankind. If so desirable a prospect is to be achieved, the apparently random variations of weather and climatic events must not only be monitored, precisely as are cyclones far out to sea, to give what warning may be possible and to allow evasive

Crevassed and eroded icebergs from the air.

action, but related to scales and models for which evidence may exist in some residual pattern of ice, oceanic sediments, or even in the concentric rings of ancient tree growth. The loyal, arduous and patient observations, and the research of the twentieth century, with its instinctive comprehension and hypotheses, will stand behind all advances. Computer imagery of weather systems matches to an extraordinary degree the most inspired guesswork of the past, such as, for instance, when meteorologists connected up sporadic readings from distant stations in what appeared, for example, inevitable isobars. I shall always cherish the memory of a weather man who said he took up meteorology because he liked drawing beautiful curves.

Doubtless the drift of continents was responsible for much of the grand planetary strategy, but Antarctica has been polar, in much the same location, for millions of years, during which there have been periods of climatic change and great variations in the build-up or the recession of the ice and, concomitantly, of the sea. The analysis of ice-cores from various depths provides evidence of age; their relative content of isotopes of gases, such as heavy oxygen-18 and the normal oxygen-16 reveals the variations of terrestrial temperatures at the time of deposition; so much more recent patterns of climatic change, if not their causes, are established.[82] The quantities of the heavier oxygen-18 in polar ice, measured in sections of sample cores, using a mass spectrometer, is directly proportional to the temperature, over a wide area of the earth, when it fell as part of the constituent molecules of water in snow. In very cold air the heavier water molecules containing oxygen-18 tend to fall out as rain or snow before reaching the higher latitudes. Will information from ice-cores eventually be related to transient weather, so that accurate long-range forecasting becomes a reality?

A prolonged period of intense cold, as we have seen, may lock up more water as ice than a milder era, with a consequent lowering of sea levels. At present they appear to be rising at a rate scarcely perceptible during the time of one or two generations of man. But, if we are moving towards the 'Little Ice Age' that has been prognosticated, then, at some point, we should expect a reversal of this trend.

Tabular iceberg, [M.C.]

A re-freezing pattern with pressure ridges between massive floes that have been welded by new ice.

The quantity of volatile theory that has been published in popular form has made common coin of an exceedingly abstruse subject. One has the suspicion that much that has been written is as ephemeral as the Antarctic is enduring. However, for most of this book I have attempted to stress the unchanging aspects, in man's time, of the great white continent. In this chapter we join the visionaries.

It is unlikely, if international stability is maintained in Antarctica—and this desirable state we shall next consider—that the meteorological and glaciological programmes will be curtailed; the continent provides too many valuable indices of past and present climatic events affecting the entire world. It is probable, for cogent reasons, that the nations will maintain their research into the upper atmosphere, their auroral, ionospheric and magnetic studies, integral to the solar wind and incoming quanta from space, and the monitoring of the polar atmospheric content of ozone, carbon dioxide and other gases. In fact, many of these areas of scientific research appear to be inter-related in the general field of atomic and particle physics.

Observatories at strategic places, from mid-Pacific to the South Pole, in estimating the increase of carbon dioxide in the atmosphere, are measuring what some scientists have called a 'greenhouse effect', its passing of solar radiation but its absorption of some of the earth's re-radiated heat. Yet this warming effect may be offset by consequent cloud formation, or by atmospheric pollution, man-made or volcanic. There is no sight yet of the end of necessary atmospheric and meteorological research.

However, there will be increasing automation of observatories. Electronic instruments, emitting pulses varying with temperature, pressure and humidity; with wind force and direction; with precipitation; with magnetic and ionospheric data; with solar and cosmic radiation; and with atmospheric composition and pollution, will be located on the surface, carried aloft in balloons, or by other means, or on buoys adrift in the immensity of the circumpolar oceans. Their output will be monitored by satellites, and their data relayed directly to world research centres. The polar-orbiting satellites, capable of providing detailed imagery—mapping land, ocean, ice and cloud, and the establishments of man—will provide continuous information about the rotating earth. What has been increasingly apparent since the middle of the twentieth century is that the comprehension of weather is a global imperative, its high cost and great benefits necessarily shared.

Mail day at the South Pole, after the arrival of the first Hercules *for the summer season.*

Emergency return in good weather. Men whose vehicle has broken down high on the antarctic plateau are towed back to base on open sledges.

A road ploughed through soft snow overlying the basic ice, near Cape Hallett, Victoria Land. It was at Cape Adare, nearby, that Borchgrevink and others made the first Antarctic landing in 1894.

Antarctic aircraft are equipped with massive ski-landing gear to facilitate landings on plateau and sea-ice. For flights from temperate latitudes to Antarctica wheel-ski—where wheels pass a short distance below the ski—allow for the transition.

The mouth of the vehicle tunnel leading down to the IGY station constructed by the USA at Byrd, 80°S., 120°W.

It was, of course, the IGY, so long ago, which first demonstrated to an astonished world that the only international treaty, that had ever held through a whole generation, concerned the scientific study of Antarctica. In those days, I was welcomed at Soviet, Australian and New Zealand, French and American bases and encouraged to examine their scientific output—fortunately, in essence, comprehensible in the universal language of mathematics—and entertained groups of men from many nations who landed out of the murk on the sea-ice or the plateau, and were able to follow our research with the appreciation of colleagues working together in a joint enterprise. The wealth of information received was multiplied in the sharing; all the co-operative nations basked in the same clear and revealing light.

It is material wealth, both terrestrial and marine, that sharing does not multiply; that may, from time to time, influence future thought and activity in Antarctica. Whenever national, rather than international, aspirations become dominant, and the old questions of territorial possession emerge, Antarctica is lit fitfully, as by the sheet lightning of a distant storm.

The conquest of Antarctica was over distance and danger; it was *terra nullius*, occupied and owned by none. It produced nothing; it held no wealth or practical incentive to settle. Cook's opinion of its grey, inhospitable desolation remained current for more than a century. To be truthful, its exploration in 'the heroic age' was motivated by the search for adventure, for personal and national honour, rather than for science. It was only after 90° South had been attained that the

121

emphasis necessarily changed and, gradually, as we have seen, all expeditions and established stations became, ostensibly at least, entirely concerned with science, attracting men and women to further observation and research in many branches of geophysics, biology, and associated sciences.

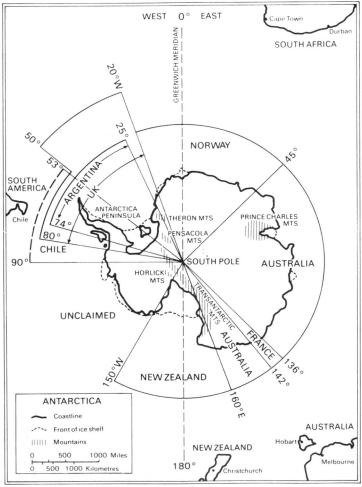

[courtesy *Australian Foreign Affairs Record*]

Claims to Antarctica remained implicit for many years. It was recognized that several of the explorers we have mentioned earlier raised their national flags and made proclamations, but, unfollowed by occupation or exploitation, these ceremonies were but words in the wind. Apart from a few gloomy islands, the ownerless oceans rolling round the southern world were the only conceivable source of wealth, and they were free to all, no power on earth able, or at that time, desiring, to curtail any predatory excess. And, in fact, the only curb that left certain creatures, whales and fur seals, hanging by precarious lines above the pit of total extinction, absolute and irreversible, was declining economic return. And this curb, in spite of all the deliberations, through the years, of international commissions,[83] the pleas of conservationists and the warnings of biologists, is the most effective persisting to this day.

Only when whales in sufficient economic quantities —measured in 'Blue Whale Units'—six seis, two fins,

McMurdo Station, on Ross Island, with Mount Erebus in background.

Helicopter operations from the Nella Dan [G.B.]

2½ humpbacks, to the one unprocurable Leviathan —were available, were the massed fleets for pelagic whaling worth their fuel, wages and maintenance. The withdrawal of most in the 1960s left to the few the reduced bounty, which even then could not cull out what was declared 'a maximum sustainable yield'. We shall return again to the future of antarctic marine exploitation, in which nations, with other international concerns in high latitudes, are still at variance.

Claims to much of Antarctica had been made before the general free-for-all, but temporary, scientific settlement of the IGY and the Antarctic Treaty was agreed upon at the end of 1959. The following table lists the longitudinal boundaries of the sectors which, in all

Blown snow provides an unusual chiaroscuro for the granite off-shore islands.

cases, include all land south of 60°S., insular or continental, to the pole at 90°S.:

United Kingdom: between 20°W. and 80°W.
    (redefined in 1962, when the Falkland Island
    Dependencies to the north were excluded).
Norway: between 20°W. and 45°E.
New Zealand: between 160°E. and 150°W.
France: between 136°E. and 142°E.
Chile: between 53°W. and 90°W.
Argentina: between 20°W. and 74°W.
Australia: between 45°E. and 160°E., excluding the
    French *Terre Adélie*.

It will be noted that the claims of Argentina, Chile and the United Kingdom overlap. In 1946–48 there were 'incidents' in the area, and a show of naval force, but the claims remain unreconciled. It is, of course, significant that several great nations—the USA, the USSR and Japan, for instance—make no claims. However, the USA and the USSR have stated that neither do they recognize the claims of others in Antarctica. Much of the Pacific sector is unclaimed.

Under the grand co-operative cloak of the IGY and the ensuing Antarctic Treaty, for thirty years, it was thought, the problems of sovereignty could be conveniently left implicit and undiscussed. However, Article IV of the treaty explicitly stated that 'Nothing in the present Treaty shall be interpreted as a renunciation of any Contracting Party of previously asserted rights or claims to territorial sovereignty in Antarctica.' Another section of Article IV agrees that 'No acts or activities taking place while the present Treaty is in force shall constitute a basis for asserting, supporting or denying a claim to territorial sovereignty in Antarctica or create any rights of sovereignty in Antarctica. No new claim, or enlargement of an existing claim to

A large sub-antarctic rookery of macaroni penguins, Heard Island.

territorial sovereignty in Antarctica shall be asserted while the present Treaty is in force.'

Only the future can show what changes, if any, will occur. One may examine the claims of the various nations and attempt to assert their relative merits. It is certain that each of the claims—though some more than others—is held in reasonable title by the historic criteria of 'taking possession': priority of discovery and occupation. It is well realized, however, that there is still no universal law or agreement that may survive the mass of men's intentions directed against it. The sovereignty of any nation over any territory still, alas, depends on the balance of power, and whether or not this is allied with goodwill and integrity.

When the Antarctic Treaty was signed all its provisions were directed towards the co-operative scientific investigation of the far south. The agreement made no provisions for exploitive interests; in fact its only material concern was for the conservation of coastal species and of the environment.

We are assured of the former contiguity of the Pre-Cambrian shield of Western Australia, with its considerable mineral wealth, and that of Eastern Antarctica, which fact makes highly probable the existence of similar mineral deposits there. However, beneath so massive an overburden of ice, the richest lodes could scarcely excite the most sanguine prospector. From all over Antarctica, wherever rock exposures occur, there have come reports of minor occurrences of minerals, but these are mere tantalizing indications of what might exist far below the ice. Furthermore, even if such mineral deposits were uncovered, the difficulties of terrain and low temperatures would create extreme physical and economic problems. Iron ores and coal exist in quantities which elsewhere on earth might attract interest: in Antarctica they would be prohibitively expensive to exploit. The formations of Western Antarctica, including the mountains of the Antarctic Peninsula, are geologically related to the Mesozoic and Tertiary Andean chain of South America, where massive copper deposits exist. It has been suggested that sulphides on the Antarctic Peninsula may eventually be worked for both their metallic and their sulphur content.

Much more tempting to speculative interests throughout the world, with the consequent lobbying of its politicians, were the reports of traces of hydrocarbons detected in holes drilled by the *Glomar Challenger*[84] in 1973, during an investigation by the USA of oceanic sediments. Originally designed for a better understanding of the Tertiary geological history of the

Tired huskies resting on dry ice, their thick insulating pelts preventing the escape of bodily heat.

Husky pups; a few teams of huskies are still retained in Antarctica, being particularly suited to travel on thin sea-ice.

Husky pups accompanying expedition men on a Sunday walk over the sea-ice to Béchervaise Island, near Mawson.

Beset! A Danish expedition vessel, strengthened for ice, the Thala Dan, *is held in heavy pack ice off the coast of Enderby Land. In this incident she was released after a week by a change in the disposition of the pressure-ice.*

A welcome from the local population. As expedition men climb down a ladder from the Thala Dan's *bows, they are met by a group of emperor penguins.*

McMurdo Sound area, subsequent operations in a three-year programme developed by the USA, Japan and New Zealand, detected the presence of gas containing 38 per cent methane.[85] On the score of safety, with an increase in temperature, and the cracking of the ice-sheet, for the teams were unequipped for 'blow-outs', drilling was concluded, and the holes were plugged with cement to prevent possible pollution.

Repercussions from the drilling have continued. Few realize the difficulties of penetrating massive moving ice to a continental shelf depressed to a depth of a hundred and fifty metres or more—twice that of other shelves, of continents unburdened with ice—let alone the maintenance of drilling rigs and platforms. It has been suggested that operations might be entirely submarine. It is inevitable that further exploration will take place, though conservation interests will naturally, and as inevitably, oppose the dangers, and these would be real, of spillage and pollution. The effects of crude oil on seals and penguins could be horrifying. In the meanwhile amongst the Antarctic Treaty Consultative Powers there will be continued debate dominated by considerations of the resources of the Antarctic Continent and its surrounding oceans.

Should any nation, under any circumstances, discover an oilfield which can operate economically, and install the highly specialized equipment necessary, overcoming difficulties never before contested, what possible effects could the operation have upon the continent which, for many reasons, I have called the 'last horizon'? I would judge that, relative to the vast continent, the area of production would be minute. It is probable that, with the backlog of the IGY and the subsequent biological programmes such as BIOMASS, the conservation interests would have a powerful, perhaps irresistible voice. And that is, I think, the only summary one could make of what may well be not far in the future. It is certain that any operation which demonstrated an ability to exploit antarctic oil would be regarded by the majority as a notable vanguard in the prolongation of our 'fossil fuel civilization'. Antarctica may perhaps remain inviolate; it must resume its ancient mantle as a terrible and beautiful white desert long after man's energy requirements have exhausted the last barrel of crude oil yielded by the vulnerable earth.

In the days when the monstrous baleen whales, the Mysticeti, roamed the southern oceans unmolested, when a hundred thousand blue whales, largest animals ever to live, rolled in the circumpolar drift, what sus-

tained their massive bodies and their great numbers? Unlike their toothed cousins, the Odontoceti, they sought for diet no fish, nor fowl, nor seal. The answer, of course, is 'krill', the astonishing little red crustacean we mention again and again, which, in countless millions graze upon the primitive plants, the phytoplankton, sea- and ice-based algae, sustained by the interaction of sunlight on inorganic nutrients. Without such photosynthesis plant and animal life would be inconceivable; its miracle is never better demonstrated, nor is there a better-balanced ecosystem than that which, by the presence of phytoplankton, existed for countless millennia in the southern oceans. It has been estimated that the baleen whales were sustained by 150 million tonnes of krill annually; the crabeater seal, living mainly at the edge of the pack ice, still accounts for 50 million tonnes, and, with the sea birds, penguins, fish and squid, themselves are eaten by the predatory

The freezing of the sea. [F.W.E.]

It has been suggested that oil drilling operations might be entirely submarine.

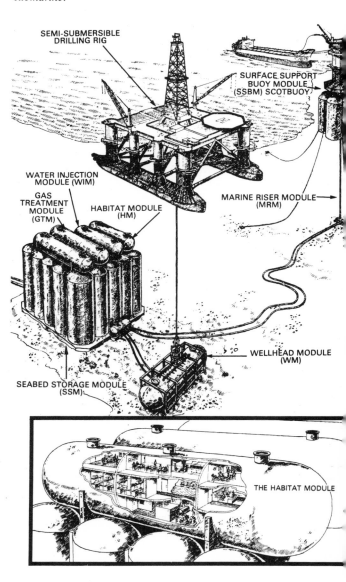

126

carnivora. So it amounts to this: after the diatomic phyto-plankton, minute unicellular seaweeds, stand as fundamental to the food cycle of the southern oceans.

When all was in balance, each member species of the nutrient chain had nearly constant population: the total available food was absorbed by a vast interdependent life-mass;[86] the average annual shares of the krill were

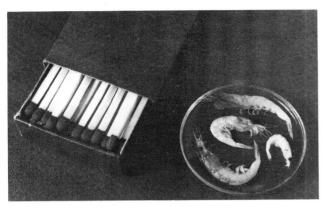

Krill. [R.R.]

Simplified food chain shows how each step in the process involves a 'diminishing return'. That is it takes 100 units of phytoplankton, such as diatoms, to grow ten units of krill, which in turn is enough to grow only one unit of its predator, the whale.

fairly constant; ultimately the only life-space for mature adults was left by their predecessors.

It was impossible to take hundreds of thousands of whales of several species, and expect natural increase to take place and keep pace. For one thing, whales in their natural state live up to fifty or more years,[87] and with such unrestrained slaughter as occurred in the first half of the twentieth century, could not possibly be self-replacing.

Any chance of their recovery now depends on three factors: the whales' protection, the availability of the krill, and the restoration of a balanced ecosystem. Already, of course, the original balance has been lost. The numbers of other than whale krill-eaters has increased: seals, penguins and other sea birds, fish and squid: none of these is food for baleen whales. So any reversal of trends must be complex and indirect. More seriously militating against the whales' recovery, however, is the arrival of a new predator: man, by whom, processed in various ways, krill may be taken directly as animal protein, or used to nourish other food sources produced in his home environments. Responsible authorities[88] have been quoted as estimating that krill trawling in the Antartic, even in the short possible season of three or four months, could provide a catch

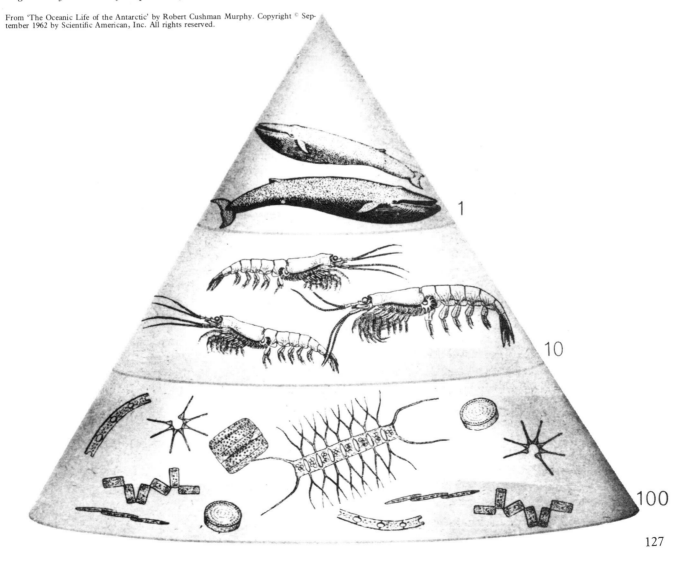

127

Wind sculpture in pressure ice, lit by a low sun.

The heraldic skua, with Dominican gulls in the background, at Heard Island.

The ice-cliff coast of Antarctica is here interrupted by high gneissic granite, affording a view of the Casey Range west of Mawson.

of 100 000 000 tonnes annually, equal in weight to the produce of the entire world's fisheries elsewhere. The same source quotes the Soviet and Japanese catch of antarctic 'cod' (*Dissostichus mawsoni*) in far southern waters, in a single year, as 340 000 tonnes, more than twice the weight trawled in the same period by British vessels working in the Iceland area. Poland was reported[89] as having harvested 30 000 tonnes of krill in 1976–77, and Japan 22 000 tonnes in the next season. Is this one-fiftieth of the potential, or are the quoted gross figures the fantasy that some have claimed?

We know too little. We look to programmes such as BIOMASS to inform us. There are and will be conventions without end. Agreement between the consultative parties, as far as on- and off-shore material resources are concerned, will continue to be prejudiced because of inevitable tensions between those who claim parts of Antarctica as their own territories, and the powerful states who do not. The twenty-first century will provide

only some of the answers; meanwhile, we have, in Antarctica, the trials and testing grounds of ideals, both national and international.

If the Pax Antarctica can be maintained, there are many aspects of the south polar regions which will be revealed in the next few decades. Tourism will certainly grow, and there is room in Antarctica for its special nourishment of the human spirit, for people to comprehend and share something of the world's greatest wilderness, to experience its grandeur and to witness its unearthly beauty. As Douglas Mawson stressed more than half a century ago, with due safeguards, there is no healthier, cleaner environment anywhere on earth. He even foresaw the day when there would be excellent scope for winter sports in high summer. Though I have experienced storm and blizzard of appalling violence, if I am to recall the calmest, most benign week I ever knew, when the sun remained unsetting, and, through

The encounter: emperor penguins on the sea-ice. Tidal levels show that the iceberg has been grounded; the incut waterline of floating icebergs will also vary as the mass of the ice is reduced by melting.

Heard Island: a volcanic peninsula projects from the glaciers of the central mountain massif. The ANARE station is just visible to the right of the small lava cones.

the crystal air, its radiant heat was a continuous benediction, when the most superb mountain ranges of virgin peaks offered a constant invitation to explore their heights, and when distant icebergs, a hundred and fifty kilometres away in the distant sea, were half hidden only by the curvature of the earth, that memory would also be of Antarctica.

Cruises on suitable vessels strengthened for ice are likely always to be expensive, but those that have occurred have offered no threat to the environment, to antarctic wildlife, or to the several historic sites visited. Doubtless, aircraft facilities will be extended, and tourist accommodation arranged, possibly in geodesic dome structures such as have been used successfully at the South Pole.[90] Should Antarctica eventually contribute to the world's resources of energy, there would be powerful arguments, salubrious and philosophical, that it could be expended in no better way than showing people the wonders of the world. There is no reason why selected areas of high scenic value, with controlled access in season to wildlife sanctuaries, should not be established for tourists and, although heating, insulation and transport costs will be high, a holiday in Antarctica should ultimately be within the reach of average overseas travellers. At many settlements, incidentally, wind or tidal power will eventually contribute substantially to local energy requirements. The electrolysis of water may provide storable, perhaps even

exportable, energy in the form of compressed hydrogen gas. If some scientific or economic enterprise eventually requires extended civilian settlement there are no insoluble problems of logistics in building such establishments. Always, in Antarctica, 'Weather and Ice are kings', and are as dangerous to the unprepared as ever they were; security will never be extended to the careless or unwary.

A popular field of speculation over many years has concerned the possible towing of antarctic icebergs to the southern continents to augment their agricultural water supplies and irrigation. Those large icebergs which reach the latitudes of the West Wind Drift have already travelled much of the distance to, for instance, Australia. Towing would pose great but not impossible strains. Several methods of getting the water ashore have been proposed. One envisages that round a suitable iceberg brought close to the coast, where it would become grounded, could be moored a plastic apron extending well below the surface and trapping fresh melt water above the undisturbed seawater below, whence it could be pumped to the land. Or, for a considerable period, water could be pumped directly from reservoirs initially melted in the iceberg itself by electric immersion heaters, as has been done to obtain fresh liquid water at some antarctic stations; or icebergs could be, conceivably, fragmented and the ice floated ashore. Informed opinion, generally, agrees to the feasibility of towing icebergs, but differs concerning the

Coastal glacier. [M.F.]

Mount Olsen, Laurens Peninsula, Heard Island.

Wind-scour.

economics. Satellite technology may be used to locate and track icebergs; that is one major problem solved. In January, 1977, an immense iceberg, ten years adrift, during which it had moved more than 3 000 kilometres, was 'photographed' near the tip of the Antarctic Peninsula, from two US satellites. It was 74 kilometres by 40 kilometres in surface area, and estimated to be 350 metres thick;[91]; sufficient water for a large city's needs over thousands of years. The typical iceberg is, of course, very much smaller; a single cubic kilometre of ice, with a top surface area of 3–5 square kilometres, might be kept moving; the twenty-first century should demonstrate whether such water transport is possible and economically viable.

For most of this book I have attempted to reveal Antarctica as an essential balance of the earth, as it has become through time inconceivable to the human mind; time so vast that it sustains the drift of continents, the evolution of species and the change of climates from one eternity to another. The glossopteris waved its green tongues in the steaming Permo-Carboniferous air. Three hundred millions of years later its fossils lie beneath the deepest ice on earth. Anything spoken of man and his aspirations, his ways of life, his buildings, ships, aircraft; his science and satellites; his economics and politics; as in this final recapitulation, is as of a single summer glaze upon the plateau surface, likely to be overlain by time much longer than man's recorded history.

131

Notes

1 'Biomass', an acronym formed from the initials of the words Biological Investigation of Marine Antarctic Systems and Stocks, is the abbreviated name of a programme of interest to several international scientific bodies. The word has assumed a useful secondary meaning. The term 'biomass' is now often used to denote the whole body of interdependent and interacting creatures indigenous to the Antarctic.

2 The Antarctic Treaty was signed on 1 December 1959 by Argentina, Australia, Belgium, the United Kingdom, Chile, France, Japan, New Zealand, Norway, South Africa, the USSR and the USA. Since 1959 seven other nations have acceded: Brazil, Czechoslovakia, Denmark, the German Democratic Republic, the Netherlands, Poland and Romania. Poland has been admitted to full 'Consultative Party' status, and may attend, with the original signatory powers, the Antarctic Treaty Consultative Meetings.

3 Antarctica could, of course, provide intermediate landing facilities for several great circle international routes between, for instance, Cape Town and Wellington or Buenos Aires and Melbourne.

4 Sastruga or zastruga (pl. -gi) is a universally accepted Russian word for a wave of wind-eroded snow.

5 Ecosystem, a major division of the whole environment in relation to living organisms (i.e. an ecological system). In fact there is no entirely independent ecosystem.

6 Krill: the whalers' name for the small crustacea, in the Antarctic especially *Euphausia superba* which occupies a basic place in the food cycle of antarctic marine animals.

7 *The Secret History of Australia—Portuguese ventures 200 years before Captain Cook* (Souvenir Press, 1977), by Kenneth Gordon McIntyre, provides an excellent general account.

8 Cook's Journal of the Second Voyage, 1772–1775, 30 January 1774.

9 *Ibid.,* 21 February 1775.

10 In long. 78° 22′E. the *Challenger's* voyage was described by Captain Scott as the nineteenth century's most important event in the history of antarctic research, after the voyage of Ross.

11 It is always noon on some meridian of longitude, as it is always midnight on that opposite it on the other side of the world. In an hour the earth turns on its axis through 15°, that is, 360° ÷ 24. Noon anywhere is easily established from the meridian altitude of the sun; the precise difference between its local time and Greenwich noon allows the calculation of longitude.

12 The fact of the 'mainland' between long. 30°W. and 170°E. being technically an archipelago with an immense overburden of ice is probably irrelevant.

13 In the next twenty years, from 1957, the USSR established five further bases. That in the South Shetlands is named Bellingshausen.

14 Long shown on US maps as the Palmer Peninsula, the area is generally now known as the Antarctic Peninsula.

15 Stuart Campbell, in charge of an Australian expedition, called briefly in 1948; and David Lewis in 1977.

16 Sabrina Coast is now the accepted name.

17 Formerly *La Coquille,* re-named *L'Astrolabe,* 1825. The first *Astrolabe* disappeared with La Pérouse, in 1788.

18 170°E. is the meridian closely parallel to the Transantarctic Mountains and the western boundary of the Ross Sea and the Ross Ice Shelf —and of the 'archipelago' extending through to the Atlantic.

19 In 1978 a party of US and NZ scientists descended deep into the crater and narrowly escaped from a minor eruption. The names of Ross's vessels, transferred to the two high peaks of Ross Island, were most apt.

20 As has been stated, Wilkes's integrity is generally undoubted and the theory has been advanced that his sightings were displaced in latitude, an error which could be explained by thick weather, faulty instruments or to an extent by acute polar mirage.

21 Most polar tents have press-studded 'trap-doors' in the fabric floors. Odours are not volatile in intense cold. Even spilt petrol in low temperatures may be inodorous.

22 Australian National Antarctic Research Expeditions.

23 It has always been somewhat inexplicable why the *Aurora* was not moored in the tried and tested anchorage in Discovery Bay. However Stenhouse had been requested by Shackleton *not* to use Scott's old wintering place, before instructions issued to Mackintosh, before the latter left England to take up his command.

24 The AAE: Australasian Antarctic Expedition.

25 The BANZARE: British-Australian-New Zealand Antarctic Research Expedition.

26 British Antarctic Territory: South of lat. 60°S. and between 20°W. long. and 80°W. long.

27 Chilean claim: Between 53°W. long. and 90°W. long.

28 Argentine claim: South of 60°S. lat. and between 20°W. long. and 74°W. long.

29 Dronning Maud Land: South of lat. 60°S. and between 20°W. long. and 45°E. long.

30 Australian Antarctic Territory: South of lat. 60°S. and between 45°E. long. and 160°E. long. with the exception of Terre Adélie.

31 Terre Adélie: South of 60°S. lat. and between 136°E. long. and 142°E. long.

32 Ross Dependency (New Zealand): South of 60°S. lat. and between 160°E. long. and 150°W. long.

33 This sector has been much explored by the USA. The USA and the USSR do not make any claims, nor recognize those existing.

34 The term 'tectonics' is often used in structural geology, to mean 'building'.

35 The Jurassic Period started 180 000 000 millions of years (±5 millions of years) and lasted about 45 000 000 years. The 'Drift of Continents' may have started in the Permian Period, 100 000 000 years earlier; estimates differ.

36 G. de Q. Robin, *Scientific American,* September, 1962.

37 The refrigeration of the Carboniferous period must have occurred long before the continental drift. Present indications are that contemporary glaciation in Antarctica is late, commencing about a million years ago. Current 'models' of the existing ice mass demonstrate a maximum age of about 200 000 years. See *Derived Physical Characteristics of the Antarctic Ice Sheet* (ANARE Interim Reports), by W. F. Budd, D. Jenssen and U. Radok, 1971.

38 As evidenced in the Vostok-Wilkes flowline, according to Budd, Jenssen and Radok, *op. cit.,* 1971. Near Byrd in Western Antarctica, the ice is younger and particles at depth may be 30 000 years old.

39 Nunatak: a rock exposure projecting above the ice or a hillock of ice owing its presence to underlying rock.

40 The apparent change of frequency of the transmission is known as the Doppler shift and is analogous to the apparent change in the pitch of a continuous train whistle or car horn, as it approaches or recedes. Passengers in a train may be conscious of the same effect when passing a level-crossing alarm.

41 Tellurometer: An electronic instrument measuring distances by the reflection time of a radar signal. The impulse and its echo travel, of course, at the speed of light. The error, in good weather, may be no more than 1 : 100 000.

42 The bare blue ice of the coastal ablation zone does absorb solar radiation in sufficient quantities to cause melting, and for a short distance inland vigorous meltwater streams may be seen near noon. Invariably they are again stilled by freezing by evening.

43 Sublimation: Ablation from the solid to the gaseous state without an intermediate liquid phase—will take place.

44 With one area west of the Amery Ice Shelf probably islanded by a deep ice-filled trench falling below sea-level.

45 For ice to form in salt water lower temperatures are required than in fresh, but, as the crystals form they exclude salt and the ice becomes an interlock of fresh-water crystals with interstitial pockets of brine. In the intense cold of the antarctic winter the

brine becomes highly concentrated and may itself crystallize, but salty ice in summer tends to extrude brine and become fresher. From old sea-ice the brine may be almost entirely leached out; water obtained from thawing it may be practically fresh.

[46] The Arctic Circle and the Antarctic Circle are placed, respectively, at 66½°N. and 66½°S. latitudes, and encircle the regions (approximately) of 'the midnight sun'.

[47] The *Fram*, designed and built by Colin Archer for Fridtjof Nansen, and used by Nansen for his famous planned drift in the Arctic ice, 1893, and, subsequently, by both Sverdrup and Amundsen. The *Fram* was designed with sloping sides, a 'saucer' to lift above, rather than to be held by, pressure ice. Now held in a special museum near Oslo, and commemorated by a model at the Scott Polar Research Institute, Cambridge, the *Fram* was one of the most successful of all early polar ships.

[48] The ice-cover of Greenland and Antarctica total, respectively, approximately 1 800 000 and 14 000 000 square kilometres.

[49] The 'tin plague' was well-known in mediaeval Europe to occur in very hard winters, when tin and pewter, very commonly used domestically, were often 'attacked'. The allotropic change from 'white tin' to 'grey tin', with accompanying expansion and disintegration, may commence at about $-8°C$ but is much hastened at lower temperatures.

[50] See note 45.

[51] The sun's rays may be reckoned as parallel because of its immense size and distance. The angles should be conceived as measured at the centre of the earth at the base of the hemispheric axis (see diagram).

[52] The sun's maximum declinations, north and south, on, respectively, the 21 June and 21 December (approximately), are inconstant within very narrow limits. It is usual to reckon the tropics to span 47° of latitude, from 23½°S. to 23½°N. See also note p. 54.

[53] Because the sun's rays are bent by atmospheric layers, particularly in high latitudes, the sun may be apparent when, without this refraction it would be invisible. Refraction must be allowed for in all astronomical observations.

[54] The sun's meridian altitude = 90°−(latitude±declination). Take the *difference* of latitude and declination if they are both north or both south; otherwise obtain their *sum*. The sun's precise declination at any time is obtainable from *The Nautical Almanac* which also lists the variable declinations of the planets and the almost constant declinations of the 'fixed' stars useful in navigation. Obviously, from an observed meridian altitude, given date, time and declination—and correction for refraction—one's latitude may be deduced.

[55] Radiant heat is transmitted through space by infra-red radiation. It may pass through air, glass or even transparent ice with little sensible heating (I have felt the benign warmth of the sun inside an igloo with clear ice windows. The solar heat is re-radiated, at longer wavelengths which the air may absorb, from the earth or rock.

[56] Dr Morton J. Rubin, US Weather Bureau, with extensive antarctic experience.

[57] Dr F. Loewe, *Journal of Glaciology*, vol 2, no 19, March 1956.

[58] Figures published in the Australian polar journal *Aurora*, Spring, 1977.

[59] Gordon de Q. Robin, The Ice of the Antarctic, *Scientific American*, September 1962, p. 140.

[60] Many attempts have been made to evaluate the 'windchill' factor in terms of the interaction of wind and temperature, and graphs ('nomograms') and, in the northern hemisphere, maps plotting regions of equal windchill for various months have been compiled. Paul Siple, the well-known US Antarctic explorer who founded the IGY Pole Station, constructed a formula to compute sensible heat loss. Some typical results are:
Exposed flesh freezes:
in minimal wind, one metre per second, at $-39°C$;
in very light breeze, 2 metres per second, at $-31°C$;
in brisk wind, 17 metres per second, at $-8°C$;
in strengthening wind, 20 metres per second, at $-7°C$.
From these figures it will be seen that even very low tempera-

tures, $-25°C$ or $-30°C$, are not dangerous for properly garbed people if there is no wind, but that much higher temperatures, with wind, may cause frostbite and be troublesome.
1 metre per second = approximately 3.6 kilometres per hour = about 2.25 miles per hour.
20 metres per second = approximately 72 kilometres per hour = about 45 miles per hour.

[61] Pressure varies as the square of the velocity, so that a wind of 80 kilometres per hour exerts sixteen times the pressure of a 20 kilometre wind.

[62] Approximately to convert kilometres to miles, multiply by ⅝; i.e. 80 km/h = 50 m.p.h. The 80 km/h wind exerts a pressure on a flat surface of 37 kilograms per sq. metre (approximately 7.5 lbs per sq. foot). The simple formula $F = .003V^2$ (where F = lbs per sq. foot and V = miles per hour) may be used for further calculations, and may, of course, with suitable conversion factors, be used for metric units.
Wind speeds are commonly expressed in metres per second.
Approximate conversions: metres per second X 2.24 = m.p.h.;
metres per second X 3.6 = km/h.

[63] *The Home of the Blizzard*, the Story of the Australasian Antarctic Expedition, 1911–1914, by Sir Douglas Mawson (London: William Heinemann, 1915).

[64] An air mass on the Equator is moving, with the surface of the earth, at about 1 600 kilometres per hour from west to east. If, as wind, it is displaced southward, it tends to maintain its west-east speed and therefore is deflected eastward as it reaches latitudes of slower radial movement. So exists the West Wind Drift in the middle latitudes of the Southern Ocean. This so-called Coriolis force deflects north-seeking winds to the west, as they reach latitudes of faster radial movement. The characteristic clockwise and anti-clockwise vortical motion of cyclones and anti-cyclones—differing in the two hemispheres—is a Coriolis effect.

[65] *Hot* and *cold* are, of course, relative terms. The Antarctic is very hot compared with, say, the boiling point of liquid oxygen ($-183°C$). The 'heat' loss of Antarctica is similarly relative.

[66] Morton J. Rubin (*Scientific American*, September 1962) calculates the annual heat energy input to Antarctica to be more than 7 000 times that represented by the world's total annual production of electricity. We should hold this fact in mind, and the whole bounty of solar energy, when we consider that still imprisoned in our depleted stores of fossil fuels.

[67] 'Geostrophic', a major wind influenced by the rotation of the earth; the term is often used to distinguish these from those with major local influences.

[68] Compiled 11 October 1965, when I was an observer with *Operation Deep Freeze*, 1965–66, at the US senior base at McMurdo Sound. More sophisticated satellite techniques, notably those established by the USA and the USSR, are continually being developed. In 1979 the NASA (North American Space Administration) *Landsat* series of satellites were in polar orbit, providing images and information on the rotating world, periodically scanned entirely during a series of passes.

[69] Temperature falls with altitude by about 6°C for each kilometre of height gained, until the fall is arrested at the level known as the tropopause, between the troposphere and the stratosphere after which the temperature increases by solar energy absorbed in reactions involving the production of ozone. These levels are variable with conditions all over the world but, in Antarctica, the tropopause is normally at about half the height or less than that—10–12 kilometres—it takes in lower latitudes, and decreases inland with the rising plateau.

[70] Such works as John Gribbin's *The Climatic Threat* (Fontana/Collins, 1978) discuss climatic change. There is, in this volume, an excellent bibliography.

[71] Sounding balloon carrying meteorological equipment which modulates radio signals transmitted back to equipment on earth, so recording air pressures, temperatures and humidities at high altitudes.

[72] The continuing development of powerful national interests in the possibilities of gaining material wealth, especially hydrocarbons and seafood, will be discussed in the final section.

73 'The Earth's Magnetic Tail', by N. F. Ness, *Journal of Geophysical Research*, vol 7, 1965.

74 *Blizzard and Fire* (Angus & Robertson, Sydney and London, 1963), by the author, gives a full account of this disaster; also of the loss of aircraft in a severe cyclone.

75 Both the plant and the amphibian existed in favourable climates in Carboniferous, Permian and Triassic times, and their presence as antarctic fossils proves the breadth of change in the continent, and its links with other land masses revealing the same fossils.

76 On Thursday, 5 January 1911 (Journal of *Scott's Last Expedition*), Ponting and two huskies narrowly escaped death when a school of killer whales shattered the floe on which they stood. Scott wrote: '. . . the facts that they could display such deliberate cunning, that they were able to break ice of such thickness (at least 2½ feet), and that they could act in unison, were a revelation to us. It is clear that they are endowed with singular intelligence and in future we shall treat that intelligence with every respect.'
In his notes on the killer whale or grampus (*Orca gladiator*), Scott recounts that in the stomach of a 21 ft. (6.401 metres) specimen were found the remains of 13 porpoises and 14 seals.

77 Several established journals publish up-to-date statistics of the whaling industry, of the workings of the International Whaling Commission, and of the recommended quotas for the various species, as may seem sustainable. Many also publish the growing body of opinion favouring conservation. The journals include *The Polar Record* (UK), *Antarctic* (New Zealand), *Aurora* (Australia), the *Geographical Review* (USA) and the Unesco *Courier*. The bulletins of the IWC are also available.

78 The study of acronyms seems essential in our time. The reader may care to substitute NSF, IOS, SCAR, SCOR, FAO, IWC, and IOC for their overt phrases. There are countless others in common use.

79 During the drift of the *Aurora*, 1915–16, many emperors were sighted, and some taken and weighed. A. H. Ninnis records the capture of five weighing 70 lb. (31.75 kilograms) average. On 10 December 1915, they 'took biggest Emperor to date . . . Weight 95 lbs, height almost 4 feet . . .'

80 The French Expedition, 1952, based at Dumont D'Urville.

81 As evidenced in *The Climatic Threat*, by John Gribbin (London, 1978). Also well illustrated in Nigel Calder, *The Weather Machine and the Threat of Ice* (London, 1974).

82 See, for instance, Nigel Calder, *ibid.* for a treatment of this theme given most concisely in his BBC television script.

83 The International Convention for the Regulation of Whaling was signed in 1946. The International Whaling Commission sets out quotas in 'Blue Whale Units' (BWU) calculated to be within the limits of sustainable yields. They have never been internationally observed.

84 The *Glomar Challenger*, in 1973, made a ten-week voyage into the Southern Ocean and the Ross Sea (where she was attended by two ice-breakers), drilling sixteen holes in the ocean bed, and taking on board for analysis almost a kilometre and a half of cores. The four holes drilled in the bed of the Ross Sea provided evidence which seemed to extend the period of Antarctic glaciation to about 20 000 000 years. Australia, formerly contiguous, it was estimated was being carried northwards still at the rate of 5–7 cm annually. The New Zealand Antarctic Society's journal *Antarctic*, for March 1973, provides a fuller account.

85 There have been many references in the popular press to these events, and the whole subject will remain in the area of highly 'volatile' news. The antarctic journals carry more sober appraisals and information, as in the article, 'Gas and cracks in ice stop McMurdo Sound drilling', in *Antarctic* (NZ), December 1975.

86 The double meaning of the acronym 'biomass' is useful.

87 Frank B. Gilbreth, *Of Whales and Women* (London, 1957).

88 'Antarctica: An Information Paper,' presented by Senator, the Hon. J. J. Webster, Minister for Science (Australia, 1977).

89 *The Age*, Melbourne, 6 March 1979.

90 The main geodesic dome at the South Pole station, Amundsen-Scott, was occupied in 1974. It is 50 metres in diameter and 17 metres high, and contains several buildings of more conventional design.

91 An excellent article, 'Iceberg Utilization', appeared in *Aurora* (Australia), 1 September 1977.

Antarctic mammals and birds

MAMMALS

Seals

crabeater seal	*Lobodon carcinophagus*
elephant seal	*Mirounga leonina*
Hooker's sea-lion	*Phocarctos hookeri*
leopard sea (sea-leopard)	*Hydrurga leptonyx*
Ross seal	*Ommatophoca rossi*
South Australian sea-lion	*Neophoca cinerea*
southern fur seal	*Arctocephalus australis* *
southern sea-lion	*Otaria byroni*
Weddell seal	*Leptonychotes weddelli*

*There are probably two or three closely related species.

Whales

blue whale	*Balaenoptera musculus*
fin whale	*Balaenoptera physalus*
humpback whale	*Megaptera nodosa*
killer whale	*Orca gladiator*
right whale	*Eubalaena australis*
sei whale	*Balaenoptera borealis*
sperm whale	*Physeter catodon*

BIRDS

Penguins

Adélie penguin	*Pygoscelis adeliae*
emperor penguin	*Aptenodytes forsteri*
gentoo penguin	*Pygoscelis papua*
king penguin	*Aptenodytes patagonica*
macaroni penguin	*Eudyptes chrysolophus chrysolophus*
ring or chinstrap penguin	*Pygoscelis antarctica*
rockhopper penguin	*Eudyptes chrysocome*
royal penguin	*Eudyptes chrysolophus schlegeli*

Albatrosses

black-browed albatross	*Diomedea melanophris*
light-mantled sooty albatross	*Phoebetria palpebrata*
wandering albatross	*Diomedea exulans exulans*
royal albatross	*Diomedea epomophora epomophora*
grey-headed mollymawk	*Diomedea chrysostoma*

Petrels

antarctic petrel	*Thalassoica antarctica*
cape pigeon	*Daption capensis*
cliff prion, fulmar prion	*Pachyptila crassirostris*
dove prion, whale bird	*Pachyptila desolata*
giant petrel, or fulmar	*Macronectes giganteus*
silver-grey petrel	*Fulmarus glacialoides*
snow petrel	*Pagodroma nivea*
Wilson's black and white storm petrel	*Oceanites oceanicus*

Gulls, Skuas

Dominican gull	*Larus dominicanus*
McCormick skua	*Catharacta maccormicki*
Southern skua	*Catharacta lonnbergi*

Terns

antarctic tern	*Sterna vittata vittata*
arctic tern*	*Sterna macrura*

*Visits antarctic waters for the southern summer.

Sheathbill

Heard Island sheathbill	*Chionis minor nasicornis*

Cormorant

blue-eyed shag	*Phalacrocorax atriceps nivalis*

Bibliography

Of the very extensive available antarctic literature, the volumes listed below comprise a representative library of the standard works in English, and a selection of contemporary writing describing the situation existing today. The list is chronological, though many recent texts may contain reappraisals of earlier expeditions and of their purposes and results. The list cannot, of course, be regarded as definitive; all the volumes mentioned will, however, be found in the larger public libraries.

1847 Sir James Clark Ross, *A Voyage of Discovery and Research in the Southern and Antarctic Regions, 1839–1843.*

1876 W. J. J. Spry, *The Cruise of H.M.S. 'Challenger'.*

1900 F. A. Cook, *Through the First Antarctic Night, 1898–1900* (*Belgica* expedition).

1901 C. E. Borchgrevink, *First on the Antarctic Continent* (expedition of 1898–1900).

1905 H. R. Mill, *The Siege of the South Pole.*

1905 N. Otto G. Nordenskjöld and J. G. Andersson, *Antarctica; or, Two years amongst the ice of the South Pole.*

1905 R. F. Scott, *The Voyage of the 'Discovery'* (2 vols).

1905 A. B. Armitage, *Two Years in the Antarctic.*

1906 R. N. Rudmose-Brown *et al.*, *The Voyage of the 'Scotia'* (Bruce, 1902–04).

1909 E. H. Shackleton, *The Heart of the Antarctic* (British expedition, 1907–09; 2 vols).

1911 J. B. Charcot (trans. P. Walsh), *The Voyage of the 'Why Not?'* (1908–10).

1912 Roald E. G. Amundsen, *The South Pole* (Norwegian expedition, 1910–12; 2 vols).

1913 L. Huxley (arr.), *Scott's Last Expedition* (vol 1: Journals of Captain R. F. Scott; vol 2: Reports of the journeys and the scientific work undertaken by Dr E. A. Wilson and the surviving members of the expedition).

1914 R. E. Priestley, *Antarctic Adventure: Scott's Northern party.*

1915 Douglas Mawson, *The Home of the Blizzard* (Australasian expedition, 1911–14; 2 vols).

1919 J. K. Davis, *With the 'Aurora' in the Antarctic, 1911–14.*

1920 E. H. Shackleton, *South* (British expedition, 1914–17).

1921 E. R. G. R. Evans, *South with Scott.*

1921 C. Markham, *Lands of Silence.*

1921 H. G. Ponting, *The Great White South.*

1922 A. Cherry-Garrard, *The Worst Journey in the World.*

1923 J. R. F. (Frank) Wild, *Shackleton's Last Voyage.*

1925 J. F. (Frank) Hurley, *Argonauts of the South . . . in the Antarctic with Sir Douglas Mawson and Sir Ernest Shackleton.*

1925 A. J. Villiers, *Whaling in the Frozen South* (Norwegian whaling expedition, 1923–24).

1928 J. Gordon Hayes, *Antarctica.*

1930 T. Griffith Taylor, *Antarctic Adventure and Research.*

1931 R. E. Byrd, *Little America: Aerial exploration in the Antarctic and the flight to the South Pole.*

1932 J. Gordon Hayes, *The Conquest of the South Pole: Antarctic exploration, 1906–1931.*

1933 G. Seaver, *Edward Wilson of the Antarctic.*

1935 Lars Christensen, *Such is the Antarctic.*

1935 R. E. Byrd, *Discovery: the Second Byrd Expedition.*

1937 R. A. Falla, *B.A.N.Z.A.R.E. Reports, 1929–31: Birds.*

1938 R. E. Byrd, *Alone.*

1938 F. D. Ommanney, *South Latitude.*

1938 John Rymill, *Southern Lights: the Official Account of the British Graham Land Expedition, 1934–37.*

1941 Russell Owen, *The Antarctic Ocean.*

1948 J. F. (Frank) Hurley, *Shackleton's Argonauts.*

1949 T. R. Henry, *The White Continent.*

1949 Finn Ronne, *Antarctic Conquest (1946–48).*

1950 Mountevans, 1st Baron (E. R. G. R. Evans), *The Desolate Antarctic.*

1951 E. W. Hunter Christie, *The Antarctic Problem: An historical and political study.*

1952 New Zealand Antarctic Society (ed. F. A. Simpson), *The Antarctic Today: a mid-century survey.*

1953 W. Arthur Scholes, *The Seventh Continent: Saga of Australian exploration in Antarctica, 1895–1950.*

1954 John Giaever, *The White Desert* (Norwegian-British-Swedish expedition, 1949–52).

1955 W. Ross Cockrill, *Antarctic Hazard.*

1955 E. W. K. Walton, *Two Years in the Antarctic* (Falkland Islands Dependencies Survey).

1957 R. G. Dovers, *Huskies.*

1957 George Dufek, *Operation Deepfreeze.*

1957 M. Fisher and J. Fisher, *Shackleton.*

1957 P. G. Law and J. M. Béchervaise, *ANARE, Australia's Antarctic Outposts.*

1958 C. Bertram, *Arctic and Antarctic: A prospect of the polar regions.*

1958 V. E. Fuchs and E. Hillary, *The Crossing of Antarctica.*

1959 Frank Debenham, *Antarctica: The story of a continent.*

1959 A. L. P. Kirwan, *The White Road: A survey of polar exploration.*

1959 Alfred Lansing, *Endurance: Shackleton's incredible voyage.*

1959 Paul Siple, *90° South: The story of the American South Pole Conquest.*

1961 R. A. Swan, *Australia in the Antarctic.*

1961 James Cook, *The Voyages of the 'Resolution' and 'Adventure' 1772–75*, edited J. C. Beaglehole.

1962 Alfred M. Bailey and J. H. Sorensen, *Subantarctic Campbell Island* (Denver Museum of Natural History).

1962 A. Grenfell Price, *The Winning of Australian Antarctica: Mawson's B.A.N.Z.A.R.E. Voyages, 1929–31.*

1962 J. K. Davis, *High Latitude.*

1963 Paul-Emile Victor, *Man and the Conquest of the Poles.*

1964 A. S. Helm and J. H. Miller, *Antarctica: The story of the New Zealand Party of the Trans-Antarctic Expedition.*

1964 Patrick D. Baird, *The Polar World.*

1964 Sir Raymond Priestley, R. J. Adie and G. de Q. Robin, *Antarctic Research.*

1967 L. B. Quartermain, *South to the Pole.*

1969 H. G. R. King, *The Antarctic.*

1972 B. Stonehouse, *Animals of the Antarctic.*

1974 D. Mountfield, *A History of Polar Exploration.*

1974 Nigel Calder, *The Weather Machine.*

1975 G. E. Watson, *Birds of the Antarctic and Sub-Antarctic* (American Geophysical Union, Washington, D.C.).

1977 L. Bickel, *This Accursed Land.*

1977 Elspeth Huxley, *Scott of the Antarctic.* Two other volumes of the same name were published in 1940 and 1966 by, respectively, George Seaver and Reginald Pound.

1978 John Béchervaise, *Science: Men on Ice in Antarctica.*

1979 J. F. Lovering and J. R. V. Prescott, *Last of Lands . . . Antarctica.*

Index